PROCRASTINATE ON PURPOSE

"Managing your time is a lot like managing your money. It's not about the numbers; it's about your behavior. The best time-management tricks in the world won't do you much good if they don't actually make your life better. In *Procrastinate on Purpose*, Rory builds on what we've all heard about time management and adds the two things that have always been missing: emotion and significance."

—Dave Ramsey, *New York Times* bestselling author
and nationally syndicated radio show host

"A brilliant insight turned into an actionable method. Start now!"

—Seth Godin, author of *Linchpin*

"We all have the same 24 hours in a day to make an impact but what if you could actually create more time? *Procrastinate on Purpose* shows how the greatest leaders in the world have figured out how to literally multiply their time. This book is a game changer."

—Jon Gordon, bestselling author of *The Energy Bus* and *The Carpenter*

"Rory Vaden has invented a way to manufacture more time in your day! This book has brilliant insights on how to become more productive in every area."

—Randy Gage, author of the *New York Times* bestseller
Risky Is the New Safe

"Rory Vaden is a contrarian—and that's a good thing. Most rail against the evils of procrastination, but in *Procrastinate on Purpose*, Vaden shows us how to use it to our advantage. In doing so, we get more of the one resource that used to be finite: time."

—John G. Miller, bestselling author of *QBQ!*, *Outstanding!*,
and *Parenting the QBQ Way*

continued . . .

"*Procrastinate on Purpose* will alter the way the professional world thinks about time—I've never read anything like it. Useful, unique, and relevant . . . this is an absolute must read for every leader."

—Sue Schick, CEO of UnitedHealthcare of Pennsylvania and Delaware

"*Procrastinate on Purpose* is the unorthodox guide for mastering time-management and productivity in our 24/7 business world. If you only read one book this year on how to become more effective and focused at work with less stress—and fewer emails—read this one."

—Jason Dorsey, cofounder of the Center for Generational Kinetics and bestselling author of *Y-Size Your Business*

"Rory's commitment to living life on purpose has challenged and inspired me again and again. In *Procrastinate on Purpose*, he shares a fresh take on time management, giving you tools and techniques that will empower you to say no to the mediocre in order to say yes to the best."

—Crystal Paine, founder of MoneySavingMom.com and *New York Times* bestselling author of *Say Goodbye to Survival Mode*

"The thing I love about Rory Vaden's books is that long before he writes about principles, he lives them. If you've ever thought, 'I wish I had more time,' read the great principles in this book. And then I dare you to do what Rory does: live them."

—Jon Acuff, *New York Times* bestselling author of *Start* and *Quitter*

"We all wish we had more time. It turns out we have plenty to spare. In *Procrastinate on Purpose*, Rory Vaden shows us how to take our time back and sets us free from the shackles of tired time-management techniques."

—Ken Coleman, author of *One Question* and host of the EntreLeadership Podcast

Procrastinate on Purpose

5 Permissions to
MULTIPLY YOUR TIME

Rory Vaden

A PERIGEE BOOK

A PERIGEE BOOK
Published by the Penguin Group
Penguin Group (USA) LLC
375 Hudson Street, New York, New York 10014

USA • Canada • UK • Ireland • Australia • New Zealand • India • South Africa • China

penguin.com

A Penguin Random House Company

Library of Congress Cataloging-in-Publication Data

Vaden, Rory.
Procrastinate on purpose : 5 permissions to multiply your time / Rory Vaden.
pages   cm
ISBN 978-0-399-17062-1 (hardback)
1. Time management.   2. Labor productivity.   I. Title.
HD69.T54V33   2014
650.1'1—dc23   2014040004

First edition: January 2015

PRINTED IN THE UNITED STATES OF AMERICA

10   9   8   7   6   5   4   3   2

Text design by Tiffany Estreicher

Most Perigee books are available at special quantity discounts for bulk purchases for sales promotions, premiums, fund-raising, or educational use. Special books, or book excerpts, can also be created to fit specific needs. For details, write: Special.Markets@us.penguingroup.com.

This book is written for those who work.
It's for the people who give every ounce of energy they have
to trying to make things better for their families,
their friends, their customers and their colleagues.

Do not grow weary, for you have a future of hope.

As for you, be fruitful and multiply;
Increase abundantly on the earth and multiply on it.

—GENESIS, 1:28

This book is dedicated to the incredible team at Southwestern Consulting.

*Thank you for your extraordinary work and for your commitment
to helping people achieve their goals in life.
You are the Multipliers of the Multipliers.*

and

*To my brother for teaching me the discipline of action;
To my dad for teaching me the value of patience;
To my wife for helping me find the right mix of both.*

CONTENTS

Part 3

The Next Step

Where I'm Coming From

You are about to radically alter the way you think about time.

And if you're like the Multipliers you're going to read about in this book, then chances are you're (justifiably) protective about what you allow to enter into your mind and whom you allow yourself to learn from.

To me personally, there is nothing more frustrating than learning something from someone who hasn't done what they are talking about.

The ideas in this book come from a variety of disciplines, but one thing you can be sure of is that they have been tested through the fire of real-life situations—including my own. Like most business books you will read, my writing includes original data from polling and statistical sampling that we have done, as well as through synthesizing existing publications and academic research.

At Southwestern Consulting, however, while we do appreciate academic research, we pride ourselves on being practitioners, and on providing strategies that are of real value and not just a pithy pitch.

In other words, these aren't just principles we have gathered from a smattering of sources and that work in theory; these are principles that we are actually practicing in our own company and learning alongside you.

I cofounded Southwestern Consulting with a few other partners in 2006. Shortly thereafter, we merged with some colleagues in London who had been working toward a similar vision since 2001. Since that time, we have grown organically to more than seventy team members and we have worked with more than seven thousand different sales teams.

Our core business is providing one-on-one accountability coaching to salespeople. At the time of this writing, we have personally coached more than twenty-seven hundred salespeople, sales leaders and entrepreneurs. That means we've been tracking the daily activity of how each of these people spends his or her time for six months or longer. When you work with people at such a close personal level for that amount of time, they are no longer just clients; they become friends.

And more than 75 percent of our "friends" say that "time management" is their biggest challenge and the reason they got into coaching. Because, you see, to a commission-based salesperson or an entrepreneur, time really is money, and it has become more difficult and stressful than ever before to keep up with the growing demands on our time. The most common phrase our clients use to describe their daily work challenges is that they feel like they are always "putting out fires." It is a challenge that we understand because every single one of our coaches—including me—is a salesperson first and a consultant second.

We all sell and service our own clients. It might be more efficient and profitable for us to have some people sell and to then just hire a team of consultants to do the coaching, but then we wouldn't know what it feels like to be in a position like our clients'. We wouldn't be practitioners. And so it is through our struggle and through all we've learned from being alongside our clients that we believe we have stumbled upon some truly unique ways of thinking differently about time. We've had to learn how to multiply our time, and this book is going to show you how to do the same—regardless of what type of profession you are in.

Although one-on-one coaching is our primary service offering, we have also tested and implemented these principles in medium-sized companies and big business as well. We've provided sales consulting to companies in twenty-seven countries. These clients range from small family-owned businesses to Verizon Cellular Sales and DIRECTV. We help companies build more of a sales culture by helping them create recruiting processes, custom sales scripts, incentive and compensation plans, custom sales, customer relationship management (or CRMs) and anything else they need to hire, train and motivate salespeople. Our U.S. corporate headquarters is in Nashville, Tennessee, and we have offices in London, Singapore and Sydney.

We know sales. We love sales. We believe in servant selling and we have for a long time.

Our parent company, the Southwestern family of companies, began in 1855 (back then Nashville was the southwestern part of the country, which is where our name comes from) and is one of the oldest privately held businesses in the United States. In 1868, our flagship sister company began working with college students, helping them finance their way through school by training them to sell Bibles and other books door-to-door during their summers. Over the last hundred and fifty years, the company has remained true to that core business, and still today nearly three thousand college students spend their school years building a team of friends and their summers selling a subscription-based web product called "Southwestern Advantage," which supplements what kids learn in school, helps parents help their kids with homework and instills the kinds of life principles contained in my books. Working with Southwestern is one of the most challenging and rigorous opportunities a young person can become involved with—and yet it is positively life changing.

Alumni of Southwestern include Marsha Blackburn (U.S. Congresswoman from Tennessee), Max Lucado (bestselling author), Jeff Sessions (U.S. Senator from Alabama), Rick Perry (governor of Texas), Ronnie Musgrove (governor of Mississippi), Mac Anderson (founder and former owner of Successories Inc.), Bruce Henderson (founder of Boston Consulting Group), Chinh Chu (senior managing director with the Blackstone Group), Donna Keene (former chief of staff for the Department of Education), and thousands more. Oh, and don't forget me—I worked in the program for four years as a recruiter and sold door-to-door for five summers, over which I earned a combined total of about $250,000 to help pay my way through college and grad school.

The Southwestern family of companies consists of more than

thirteen different business units in different industries, including the number one Raymond James financial planning office in the world, one of the fastest growing direct sales companies (Wildtree), and the largest school fund-raising company in the world (Great American). All together we have more than four million customers a year and generate several hundred million dollars in revenue.

At Southwestern, our mission is simple: to be the best organization in the world at helping people develop the skills and character they need to achieve their goals in life. So while there are many things that we do as a corporate family, the primary reason we exist is simply to help people achieve their goals in life.

Let's start with yours . . .

Part 1

The Truth About Time

1

What You Thought You Knew

Everything you know about time management is wrong.

That is the premise we started from as we began the journey of trying to answer the question "How do the most successful people today choose to spend their time?"

After working with more than seven thousand different teams in twenty-seven countries and coaching more than twenty-seven hundred people one-on-one in their daily lives for six months or longer in the past eight years, our team at Southwestern Consulting has validated that premise.

Successful people think differently. And it is their thinking that shapes a different set of choices they make, which ultimately yields incredibly different results from the rest of us.

The most popular frameworks that the majority of the working world uses to understand, discuss and dissect time management have either been drastically enhanced or completely discarded by the people who most effectively *multiply* their time.

Why do these people think differently?

It's not because they wanted to; it's because they had to.

> *Creating the next level of results requires the next level of thinking.*

It's because these Multipliers have realized that creating the next level of results requires the next level of thinking.

It's because the pressure to produce results has increased, but so have the tools available to us to achieve those results.

It's because they know that, as it relates to the demands on our time, things have changed.

Consider a given day . . .

We get up. We get ready. We run errands. We pay bills. We do housework. We cook. We eat. We clean up. And then we get ready for bed. These tasks alone can tally as much as five hours of time a day. It was reported in *Newsweek* that the average person spends one hour a day . . . looking for stuff!

When you add in the routine daily work tasks, the number of hours grows even larger. We recently did a six-month analysis of more than eight million e-mails coming into companies from a half-dozen different industries, and found that the *average* executive gets 116 e-mails every single working day.* Obviously, however, it's not just e-mails we have to keep up with. Voice mails.

---

*Southwestern Consulting e-mail traffic analysis of family of companies for September 2013 through February 2014.

Text messages. Meetings. Conference calls. Paperwork. Reports. Social media updates. It's not uncommon for working professionals to spend more than three hours every day keeping up with the basic routine activities—before we even get any real *work* done.

The result is that a new form of procrastination runs rampant. Quickly and quietly it has engulfed the workplace like a swarm of killer bees, creating a host of insidious problems:

- Stifled innovation
- Employee turnover and burned-out human capital
- Perpetuating miscommunication
- Failing projects and missed deadlines
- Disengaged and underutilized team members
- Wasted potential and a culture of overwhelming speed, stress and anxiety

These are just a few of the destructive by-products of this phenomenon that cost organizations millions of dollars each year. Not to mention the years of an individual's life that are taken by the pressure that it creates.

Pervasive and powerful, this productivity killer and new form of procrastination is the most expensive invisible cost in business today . . .

Priority Dilution

Unlike traditional procrastination, Priority Dilution has nothing to do with being lazy, apathetic or disengaged. Yet it is the same net result: We delay the day's most important activities by consciously or unconsciously allowing our attention to shift to less important tasks.

Ironically, Priority Dilution affects the top performers and the chronic overachievers, the people who are well intentioned and *trying* to do their best job. Because of their extraordinary competency, however, these people typically have more and more responsibility dumped on their plate until they eventually overload.

To someone struggling with Priority Dilution, it can sometimes feel like the harder they work, the more they fall behind. For every e-mail they send out, they get two in return. And each task they complete seems to hold behind it two more additionally that need to be done.

> *The amount of busy work always expands to fill the amount of time we allow to be available.*

While they work incredibly hard, they seem to find that the Parkinson's Law is also true: "The amount of busy work always expands to fill the amount of time we allow to be available."

Their life is often characterized as a constant state of interruption. The most common phrase they use to describe their situation is delivered with a hint of hopelessness in their voice as they plead, "It just seems like I'm constantly putting out fires."

They are spread thin. Overwhelmed. Under-rested. And they feel like they are falling further and further behind. Unsure if they can keep up with the pace that life is throwing at them, they operate under a dark cloud, sometimes desperately asking themselves in the back of their mind, "Is this ever going to get better?"

If it sounds like I know this person well, it's because I do; it's me.

Unlike many of my fellow writers, researchers, speakers and "experts," being an author isn't my "real" job. I am an entrepreneur, a salesperson, a sales manager and an executive with a team of now more than seventy people whom I'm trying to serve every day. And while the success of my first book, *Take the Stairs*, has suddenly made me into an international author, I never thought I was going to write a book on productivity.

That's because I never set out to solve the world's time-management problems; I set out to solve my own.

Let's start by talking about everything I *thought* I knew . . .

I thought I was *so* busy

For years I had convinced myself that I was *so* busy. I would even make mini presentations to myself in my own mind about how I *must* be "busier" than most people around me.

I would even tell people, "I am just *so* busy right now." Over and over people would ask me how I was doing and I would reply with the same melodramatic sigh that communicated just how overwhelmed I was.

It was almost as if I was allowing myself to perpetuate this story that I was so busy because it gave me some false sense of importance about myself. Sad.

Then suddenly out of the blue, one day it occurred to me that the most successful people I knew *never* complained or even spoke about how busy they were. More than that, they never even seemed to let on to anyone about everything they had going on in their lives.

These were people who were at least as "busy" as me, and who had more responsibilities than I did.

So I asked one of them about it once and she said, "You reach a point where you realize how futile it is to expend energy sharing or even thinking about how 'busy' you are. Once you get to that place, you shift to focusing that energy productively into getting the things done rather than worrying about the fact that you have to do them."

I noticed that they weren't necessarily working less than me; but they had a peace about them that I didn't. It was a sense of peace that resulted from their acceptance of their own situation.

What did I take from that?

Quit telling everyone how busy you are. Resist the indulgence of saying "I am too busy."

Your problem is not that you are too busy; your problem is that you don't own your situation.

You get stressed and frustrated with distractions, fine—we all do. But your life is your responsibility. Any commitments you have were either made or allowed by you.

It's not even right to complain or whine to others about how busy you are. You and I have the same amount of time in a day as Gandhi, Dr. Martin Luther King Jr., Mother Teresa, Michael Jordan or anyone else who has achieved greatness.

Once you own your problem, you empower yourself to create your own solution.

Once you own your problem, you empower yourself to create your own solution.

So the first step is to get over our self-indulgent complaining about how we're so busy or there just isn't enough time in a day. If you are saying those things to yourself, then you are allowing yourself to be a victim—like I was.

You are not a victim. You are in charge. You are capable. You are powerful enough to decide what you will and won't do with your time.

But one thing you are not is too busy.

This is just the first of several ways that Multipliers think differently.

I thought "balance" was the standard

It seems like the most common encouragement we hear from "time-management experts" is the importance of work–life balance.

Yet, the more time we've spent around Multipliers, the more we've come to realize that balance is crap.

The concept of balance is not only a discordant metaphor for how to spend your time, but an ineffective strategy. Striving for "work–life balance" is an impractical standard; it's one that won't bring you the results you truly seek—and it should be avoided.

By definition, balance means "equal force in opposite directions," which implies that to be *balanced*, our time and energy should be spread in a perfect distribution across various tasks we have in our life. But if we sleep eight hours a day and work eight hours a day, then to truly be balanced we could only do one other activity and it would have to be eight hours every day. That concept is absurd and outdated.

Success in business, at home and in life doesn't come from applying our resources proportionately throughout different areas. In fact, it's just the opposite. Success usually is the result of focusing our talents, money, time or energy in one priority direction for a shorter period of time to create a desired result, which in *Take the Stairs* I called a "season." In one word, a "season" is best defined as "imbalance."

- For example, if you were thousands of dollars in debt, you wouldn't get out very fast if you were only paying off an extra ten dollars per month more than your minimum balance. You'd have to find a way to make sacrifices in other areas of your life to throw more and more money at your debt problem until it was gone.

- If you were two hundred pounds overweight, you likely wouldn't get the transformation you wanted by working out ten minutes per week. Instead, you'd have to arrange your life for a while so you could work out more like ten hours per week to get you to an acceptable level of health.

- An entrepreneur would take forever to get her business off the ground by working just thirty minutes per week on the side. If the effort was going to be significant, it would take much more time than that to get it started.

The beauty of *imbalancing* your resources in one direction for a short period of time is that once you create your desired result, it is usually much easier to *maintain* that level of performance postseason. It becomes comfortable to consistently stay in the new range and usually requires much less effort and/or little thinking at all.

A panoramic view of a season and postseason leads us instead to the strategy that we like to call "working double-time part-time for full-time free time."

- Once you get out of debt and you have no monthly payments, it's much easier to get rich and stay out of debt.

> *Working double-time part-time for full-time free time.*

- After you get into shape, it's pretty easy to stay in shape working out just a couple times a week and having only a semi-strict diet.
- A successful business should eventually become a revenue-producing asset for the owner, with only fractional time spent managing it once all the necessary systems and people to make it run have been implemented.

As I sit right now writing this book, I have blocked off five days of virtually ignoring everything else in my life because I know that this work in and of itself is a Multiplier for me. And I know that the very endeavor of this book is one that is best produced through a short *season* of intense focus and not a sentence or two written every day for a lifetime.

All of these are examples of the payoff resulting from embracing a "double-time part-time for full-time free time" strategy. The metaphor of a "season" not only makes more practical sense when applied to every area of daily life, but it is also the actual practice of "well-balanced," high-performing people (Multipliers).

Meanwhile, "balance" is more often an excuse for justifying underperformance than a valid explanation for why we're not achieving the results we want in the different areas of our life. Balance is not a benchmark you should be measuring yourself by and it's not a standard that will bring you a life you love.

Embrace the *season*. Embrace the *focused imbalance*. Embrace working double-time part-time and you shall soon embrace the full-time free time.

I thought "leisure" was the goal

I'm not sure where I got this idea from, but a substantial amount of the stress I was experiencing in my life was the result of my thinking that "leisure" and "retirement" were the ultimate goals of a happy life.

Maybe it was from the baby boomer mindset of "If you work hard enough, then one day you get to retire!"

Maybe it was the entrepreneurial dream of my venture capital friends saying, "It only takes one great idea and you can be rich by the time you're thirty!"

Maybe it was the escalator mentality of an entitled younger generation always convinced there is a shortcut or an easy way.

Whatever it was, though, that gave me the idea that permanent leisure as the ultimate goal was incredibly wrong.

> *Whatever it was, though, that gave me the idea that permanent leisure as the ultimate goal was incredibly wrong.*

Have you ever taken a ten-day cruise? Have you ever been bedridden for a few weeks or even a few days? Do you know anyone who retired at thirty?

If so, then you know there are only so many margaritas you can drink, so many hours of catching up on sleep and so many reruns you can watch before something awful happens . . . you get bored out of your mind!

I am all about working hard and enjoying your payoff. I believe in pursuing a smarter and better way. I am a supporter of pursuing your dreams and manifesting your ideas into reality. I am an advocate of making time to do the things you enjoy. And I certainly believe in the value of having more money than you know what to do with. But it took me spending time with real Multipliers to realize that work isn't something to be endured, that we should try to avoid whenever possible, and it isn't something that should have a finish line that you race to so one day you can stop.

Work is a fundamental part of life and a source of deep satisfaction. We were created to work. Work produces happiness and great rewards that fill our lives with joy. Work is one of the most honoring forms of worship that we have!

Not only were we created to work, we've been instructed and warned about the dangers of *not* working. Do you know that according to a 2012 Nielsen report, the average person over the age of sixty-five watches forty-eight hours of television per week? That is nearly seven hours a day!* That doesn't sound very rewarding, if you ask me.

---

*David Hinckley, "Americans Spend 34 Hours a Week Watching TV, According to Nielsen Numbers," *New York Daily News*, September 19, 2012, nydailynews.com/entertainment/tv-movies/americans-spend-34-hours-week -watching-tv-nielsen-numbers-article-1.1162285.

Being a great parent takes work. Being a great leader takes work. Being great at anything takes work. Whom do you look up to who *doesn't* work at anything in their life, or never worked for the good of another person? Who is there worth emulating who does not work?

No one.

Why, then, do we subscribe to this myth that somehow our lives would be better if we had less work?

It's another misleading misconception that we carry in the back of our minds, holding ourselves up as failures and examples of how we aren't living the right life just because we are *working* a lot.

I love how author Timothy Keller describes the goodness of our work in his book *Every Good Endeavor*:

> *The book of Genesis leaves us with a striking truth—work was part of paradise.*
>
> *. . . We so often think of work as a necessary evil or even punishment. Yet we do not see work brought into our human story after the fall of Adam, as part of the resulting brokenness and curse; it is part of the blessedness of the garden of God. Work is as much a basic human need as food, beauty, rest, friendship, prayer, and sexuality; it is not simply medicine but food for our soul.*

Regardless of your spiritual beliefs, I hope you can see the value in this attitude toward work, because it mimics the same view that ultra-performing Multipliers have—regardless of their religious faith.

I am not saying that life should *only* be about work. But proper and appropriate amounts of work are a critical part of a satisfied life.

Work is integral.

Work is freedom.

When done the right way, work is joy.

I thought "being effective" was the highest pursuit

Efficiency is doing things right, but effectiveness is doing the right things.

This catchphrase common in the productivity field was one of the first and is still one of the most frequent things I've ever heard about time management. Since I hear it repeated often, I began to wonder if ultra-performers really agree with it?

As it turns out, for the most part they do. But there is something missing.

First of all, it is peculiar how this popular cliché has given somewhat of a bad name to efficiency. Defined as "performing or functioning in the best possible manner with the least waste of time and effort," efficiency still seems like a very worthwhile pursuit. For individuals and organizations, it certainly is nothing to shy away from, since it has an incredible cost savings.

The more fascinating discussion, though, is around the topic of effectiveness.

Effectiveness is from the Latin root word *effectus*, meaning "to bring about, to make or do," and its actual dictionary definition is given as "competent and able to perform well; having a proven capacity; adequate to accomplish a purpose; *productive of or capable of producing a result."*

Effectiveness, as defined by the catchphrase, is apparently only *part* of the story. One of the defining characteristics of Multipliers is their relentlessly strong focus on *results*. In fact, one of the most defining characteristics of financially successful people is that they actually choose to be paid based on their results, rather than their time.

Wealthy people understand an inherent relationship between risk and reward. While it's not *always* true that the greater the risk, the greater the reward (there are plenty of risky stupid things that people do that have little likelihood of reward), it is true that the biggest rewards will always include risk and uncertainty.

The number one risk that rich people are willing to take is to be paid for their results rather than or in addition to their time.

They choose to take a chance on themselves. They believe in their own self-discipline and their own ability to produce results.

- Venture capitalists sink big money into something when it is basically just an *idea* because they believe in the ability of themselves and their team to create results that will pay out massive dividends.
- Salespeople invest time and energy into making sales calls in hopes that they will eventually be able to make commissions that pay a great hourly rate and that they will get referrals that will help their business grow and grow and grow.
- Executives take on roles that require them to make tough decisions on uncertain futures because they expect to be rewarded on the bottom-line profits that result from their

discernment. Good choices equal more money; poor choices equal less money.

- Entrepreneurs risk their livelihood for the chance of controlling their own destiny by paying themselves last after all the other people and expenses in the company are paid.
- Recruiters in direct sales companies forego traditional salaries in the conviction that if they can help enough other people be successful, it will come back to them many times over.

These are just a few examples of Multipliers who risk a lot to (they hope) be rewarded a lot at a later date.

Yes, these people sometimes lose and lose big; but they also win big because they take a chance on themselves. They win rewards because they risk losses.

But the common theme in all cases is that they are paid for their results. They aren't paid for their activity. They aren't paid for their time. They aren't paid for their effort. They aren't paid for their competency, capacity or even ability. They simply and clearly are paid for their results.

The key distinction is that to a Multiplier, success isn't so much about efficiency *or* effectiveness; it's about efficacy.

"Efficacy" is defined as "the quality of being successful in producing an intended result."

> *The key distinction is that to a Multiplier, success isn't so much about efficiency or effectiveness; it's about efficacy.*

Admittedly there is some discrepancy about how closely synonymous all three of these words are (efficiency, effectiveness and efficacy), and if there is really a strong enough difference among them to draw a true delineation; but really that is a matter of semantics.

What is significant is that to a Multiplier, it isn't enough to be "competent and able to perform well" or to be "capable of achieving a result"; it only matters that we *actually* create the results we intended.

To them it's not *necessarily* about doing things right.

And it's not *completely* about doing the right things.

Truly, it's not about getting *things* done at all.

To a Multiplier, it is ultimately *only* about producing their desired results.

Too many times we have a focus on all that we *did* instead of all that *resulted from* what we did.

Too many times we convince ourselves that if we are doing something, then we are working.

Too many times we soothe ourselves with the false sense of satisfaction from all the thought and time we put into something when it didn't produce any significant result.

So you see, as it turns out:

Being busy is not a virtue.

Balance is bogus.

Leisure is not the ultimate finish line.

And effectiveness isn't what really matters.

Everything you know about time management *is* wrong.

And that's just the beginning . . .

Chapter Summary

What You Thought You Knew

KEY POINTS

- Priority Dilution is the new procrastination. It often affects the chronic overachievers.
- Many of the most common catchphrases we hear in relation to "time management" are not views shared by true Multipliers.

UNEXPECTED FINDINGS

- Telling yourself and others how "busy" you are is a self-defeating pattern that erodes your feeling of ownership and control and thwarts your creativity from being used to find solutions to your challenges.
- Balance is a myth that doesn't even make practical sense to pursue. A Multiplier's viewpoint is one of *imbalancing* their focus and energy in a desired direction for a short amount of time to create a desired result.
- Leisure is a deceptively unsatisfying goal. Work is good and should be one of the primary sources of joy in our lives.
- Results are what matter, and they are what Multipliers keenly drive toward. If you focus on producing results without limiting your ideas about how to create those results, you will come up with amazing solutions.

STARTLING STATISTICS

- The average person spends one hour a day looking for stuff.
- The average person over the age of sixty-five spends forty-eight hours per week watching television.

ACTION QUESTIONS

- What if you erased everything you thought you knew about time management?

2

Managing and Prioritizing Your Time

Aprofessor had a glass jar sitting at the front of his class with large rocks in it up to the top. He asked, "Class, is this jar full?" To which they all replied, "Yes, of course it is."

The professor then took a handful of pebbles from behind his desk. When he dropped them into the jar, they sifted in and around the rocks. He then asked, "Class, is this jar full?" And then with a smile they all nodded: "Okay, okay, now it's full."

From underneath a table the professor then pulled a cup of sand and poured it into the jar. It filled in comfortably around both the rocks and the pebbles. And so the professor asked once more, "Class, is this jar full?" Now realizing that it couldn't possibly be filled any further because there was no visible space, they said, "Okay, now it is definitely full."

Yet again from behind his desk the professor pulled out another element. This time it was a pitcher of water and he poured it in, filling in the last remaining space in the jar. He then turned to his class and said, "As in life, we often think we can do no more; but when we push to be creative, we find that there is always room for us to fill."

That story is probably one of the oldest in the personal development world, yet I've never heard of another metaphor that more accurately depicts the strategy for managing your time.

This illustration is the epitome of the efficiency argument. It highlights how there is almost always a way to fit more in. And that seems to fit very well in line with traditional "managing your time" thinking because that paradigm was all about developing tools and techniques to help us get the *most* amount of tasks done in a single day.

The general body of work in the area of time management is mostly about being efficient and it is true that if we were able to do our existing work more efficiently then that should create margin to do other additional things.

It is a linear form of thinking, and as mentioned earlier there is still, more than ever, incredible value and cost savings to be reaped from learning to do existing things more efficiently.

The only real weakness of the rocks, pebbles, sand analogy is that it doesn't allow for an important part of reality. In other words, it is a nice story with a truly valuable lesson but it doesn't completely parallel the dynamics of modern day life.

In the demonstration everything fits nicely into the cup if you *organize* it the right way and put in the elements in the appropriate order. But in the real world you can be *perfectly* organized and still run out of capacity to fit more in. Not to mention that the goal is not *necessarily* to fit more in! Remember, the goal is simply to *produce more results*.

But to use the same analogy, let's suppose that the jar represents the twenty-four hours in your day and the pitcher of water represents everything there is to do. Only this time let's say that you reached *absolute maximum efficiency* in every single thing you did during the day and so you didn't even have "rocks" to put in your jar; everything was water.

What you would eventually find is that no matter how well you "managed your time" and no matter how *efficiently* you worked, the jar of your day would eventually overflow.

THINGS TO DO

YOUR DAY

Why?

Because of an obvious truth but one that is worth articulating . . .

> *There is* more *to do than you can* ever *do.*

There is *more* to do than you can *ever* do. There is always *something* else that you *could* do. There are always more improvements you can make. There is something additional that you can add. There is some other place that you can go. Et cetera.

Again, efficiency is very much still worth incorporating into our lives. However, because of that inevitable truth that there is always more to do than you can ever do, the *efficiency* paradigm and the "managing your time" argument eventually caps out; its benefit is limited. The jar of overflowing water in this modified example is a strong visual representation of how we find many of our coaching clients, consulting clients and research subjects *feeling*.

They are working faster than they ever have in their entire life. They are working longer than they ever have. They have more advanced tools and technology. They are pushing harder—and yet they are stressed, overwhelmed, pressured and sometimes they feel like they are falling further and further behind each day. "Their cup runneth over"—but not in the good way.

That is because they are still operating in linear, one-dimensional thinking, which is, "if I can move faster, I can fit this all in." It's not that there is anything wrong, bad or incorrect about moving faster—the ability to outwork others counts for a lot and was a major focus of *Take the Stairs.*

But those who still believe that more hours or more efficiency is the ultimate answer to their workload challenges have sentenced themselves to perpetual stress because they haven't yet acknowledged that it is a never-ending wheel—and in the end a nonwinning stance.

In fact, for many such individuals, the very reason they are stuck in that old paradigm is because to change out of it would feel like they are admitting defeat. They would rather be miserable than admit they need to change.

Part of the reason so many people are stuck in the linear, one-dimensional thinking of time management and efficiency is because the actual semantics of the phrase "time management" reinforces that type of thinking.

"To manage your time" suggests that you should work faster to fit more in, in the time that you have. Another way of saying it is "to make use of your time." And that is exactly what we are doing when we are being efficient, we are getting the most *activity* out of the time that is available.

But here is the truth: You can't *really* manage time.

Everyone talks about our "time-management" skills. You may have even picked up this book because you think you have room for improvement or you're curious about "time-management" strategies. "Time management" might very well be what you think you've gotten yourself into here with this book, but you haven't.

Because there is no such thing as time management; there is only self-management.

> *There is no such thing as time management; there is only self-management.*

You can't manage time. You can't control time. You can't start time. You can't stop time. You can work fast or slow, but time carries on at the exact same rate regardless of what you or I want or do.

You can, however, manage yourself. You can choose what you do today with the time you've been given. You can decide which things are worth investing yourself in and which are not.

You can choose to either be focused on things that matter or allow yourself to be swept away in a sea of distraction.

You do have control over yourself. And once you grasp this truth, you are ready to "Prioritize your time."

THE CRITICAL DIFFERENCE

MULTIPLIER MINDSET CASE STUDY

Tracy Christman, Franchising, Budget Blinds

Orange, California

With more than 70 percent of women in the labor force, "working mom" is a very common reality these days; but to Tracy Christman, that doesn't mean having to choose between being *either* a successful parent *or* a successful employee.* As the vice president of vendor alliance for Budget Blinds, she rounds out a team of nine very sharp, savvy and service-minded individuals who make up the executive team at Home Franchise Concepts (the parent company of Budget Blinds and Tailored Living).

---

*U.S. Bureau of Labor Statistics, "Employment Characteristics of Families Survey," April 25, 2014, bls.gov/news.release/famee.nr0.htm.

For more than twelve years, Tracy's role literally and regularly has taken her around the world as she develops and maintains relationships with suppliers and vendors who are mission critical to the success of the exponentially growing organization. As you might imagine, this has created quite a conflict at times for this mother of two.

"Honestly, I've always struggled with the pull between work life and home life. My number one priority and desire is to be a great mom, so perhaps there have been times where I've worked a bit too much," Tracy humbly admits. "But I've come to embrace that struggle as just one more challenge of life that you have to work through, and my family and my colleagues have always rallied around to support me."

She continues, "My husband and I sat down early on and made a decision that we'd work together as a team to make sure I could be a high performer at work and still never miss a special function for the kids. We've wanted to make sure our kids know they are number one, and even they have been flexible with me to help make that happen because we've always found special ways of connecting.

"When they were young, if I was going out on the road, I would always buy two books—one for them and one for me. As an immovable and uncompromised appointment, I would then call them at the same time every night before bed and we'd read together. We had *real* conversations about important things—which, looking back, we might never have even had if I had been physically present at home. And whenever I came back from a trip, we'd block out time so that I could show them pictures of all that I was doing so that we had a chance to experience it together.

"Really, the fact that I do things a hundred and twenty percent and I've probably taken too much on my plate at times has proven to be one of the greatest blessings in my life for helping me to be better at prioritizing. It helped me learn to get comfortable saying no to things when it was appropriate, because I had to in order to protect the time with my kids. Similarly, it forced me to elevate my organization and processes by which I manage projects at work to levels that I likely would've never reached without those pressures. This constant struggle has strengthened my ability to clearly and quickly evaluate—at any given moment in my personal or my professional life—'what is the next thing I can do that is going to *truly* make a *critical difference*?'"

As with most Multipliers, Tracy seems to be thankful for the challenges that time places on her and grateful for the good fortune she's had along the way. Whatever she's doing must be working because now, at ages sixteen and twenty, her children are amazing young adults and that "small" company she helped build has grown from a hundred and ten franchisees to more than a thousand.

I refuse to let my kids or my family be the reason why I can't achieve excellence at work; rather they are the reason why I must.

Tracy summarizes our time together with a powerful series of statements: "I'm simply not going to sacrifice being a good mom *or* being a key part of our mission serving our franchise owners at work. One thing I've never understood is how some people cite their kids as the reason it's not possible for them to be great in their career. I refuse to let my kids or my family be the reason why I can't achieve excellence at work; rather they are the reason why I *must*."

Prioritizing your time

Once you admit to yourself that you can't manage time and that you can only manage yourself, and you accept that there is more to do than you can ever possibly do, a new strategy emerges: prioritizing.

"Prioritize" is defined as "to arrange or do in order of priority," and "priority" is defined as "the state or quality of being earlier in time, occurrence."* Combined that would read something like "to arrange or do in order of time or occurrence."

I assimilated that to create my own shorthand definition of prioritizing: to put one task in front of another.

And oh, how there is so much value to learning how to put one task in front of another! Like efficiency and managing your time, this too has incredible application to our lives.

In the past twenty-five years or so, it seems that there has been a lot more focus on prioritizing, which I believe was largely spurred by the widespread adoption of the late great Dr. Stephen R. Covey's book, *The 7 Habits of Highly Effective People.* An international best seller of more than twenty-five million copies

---

*Dictionary.com, "prioritize," dictionary.reference.com/browse/prioritize?s=t.

worldwide, Dr. Covey's book has affected and impacted the positive trajectory of the lives of so many—including my own.

Chapter three of the book was called "Put First Things First," and became the seminal work on redefining the way the world looked at time. Prioritizing and effectiveness became synonymous, as Dr. Covey seemed to clearly state to the world for the first time, "The key is not to prioritize what's on your schedule, but to schedule your priorities."*

Then he presented a tool to help us realize that not all tasks are created equal. This tool has become so pervasive it's almost impossible to have a conversation about productivity without talking about it. Dr. Covey referred to it as the "Time-Management Matrix."

It was a simple graph where the y-axis represented Importance and the x-axis represented Urgency. Graphically, it created a natural separation into these four distinct quadrants, which represent four different types of tasks in our lives:

1. Important and Urgent
2. Important but Not Urgent
3. Not Important but Urgent
4. Not Important and Not Urgent

Chances are, since you're reading this book you're at least familiar with the chart I reference above and fully aware of its

---

*Dr. Stephen Covey, *The 7 Habits of Highly Effective People* (New York: Free Press, 1989).

power. (And if you haven't read Dr. Covey's book I highly recommend you do so.)

The primary appeal that Dr. Covey was making was that results come by focusing on quadrant 2 (Important but Not Urgent). These are things like planning your strategy, relationship building, and recognizing and investing in new opportunities.

The challenge for most of us, though, is that we would give up these quadrant 2 activities by accidentally allowing ourselves to be sucked into the quadrant 1 (Important and Urgent) activities.

Part of the brilliance of the matrix was that it created a *two-dimensional* model for thinking about and deciding how we spend our time. While efficiency is a linear decision-making model (how can I speed things up to fit more in?), the Time-Management Matrix has two factors to consider in our calculation of how we spend our time: Importance and Urgency.

This framework and the strategy of prioritization seemed to shift everything from only a focus on being more efficient and moving faster, to instead being effective by focusing first on what matters most.

Being effective by focusing first on what matters most.

I have to wonder if some of his ideas were influenced by the powerful essay written in 1967 by Charles Hummel called the "Tyranny of the Urgent."*

Both Mr. Hummel and Dr. Covey seemed to be targeting this undeniable challenge that most of us have fallen victim to—what

---

*The essay in its entirety can be accessed at navfusion.com/assets/Tyranny%20of%20the%20Urgent%20%5BHummel%5D.pdf.

our modern-day coaching clients would describe as "putting out fires."

It is obvious that this is still the preeminent and pervasive challenge the working world faces as it relates to choosing how we spend our time. Part of how I know is because I seem to have inadvertently coined a phrase in *Take the Stairs* that aptly described and pinpointed this dynamic and the struggle we all have with it: Priority Dilution, or PD.

Ironically, nearly every single item of major national media and publicity coverage for *Take the Stairs* showed an apparent fascination with and recognition of the accuracy of the phrase "Priority Dilution." (Which, as a side note, is what ultimately led to me writing this book you're holding now, as it wasn't a part of our original plan.)

Allow me to revisit the visual representation of the pitcher of water as it relates to how we spend our time.

This time, let's say that the pitcher of water doesn't represent the tasks that you have to do, but now it represents the 168 hours in your week you have to *spend*. The way you decide to *spend* that time is by using the four quadrants and calculating which things are most important and most urgent.

For simplicity's sake, let's say that you are going to distribute your time across the various areas of your life. We'll use the same six areas, in no particular order, that I referred to in *Take the Stairs* in the section on living a Five-Star life:

- Family
- Faculty (Work)

- Faith
- Fitness
- Fun
- Finances

And since we are talking about prioritizing, let's have one glass represent each area of your life, like this:

168 HOURS/WEEK

FAITH   FAMILY   FITNESS   FUN   FACULTY   FINANCES

Remember, the power of prioritizing is to "put one task in front of another." It's consciously choosing (by way of a calculation using criteria such as the time-management matrix or some other method) which activity you are going to focus on first. So you are going to spend your time on your "priorities" first.

Let's just say your priorities *were* in the order of what's above. After taking out water for the amount of time you sleep, then what's left over you'd divide among some number of priorities until you had no time left. It might look something like this:

168 HOURS/WEEK

FAITH   FAMILY   FITNESS   FUN   FACULTY   FINANCES

I will admit that although I am a natural skeptic, I do have an appreciation for the eternal optimist saying, "I'd find a way to fill all my glasses up!" And while trying to find a way to have *both* and focusing on creating the desired result *is* the right *thinking*, it doesn't really fit here as a viable plan. Because no matter how long your perspective is, we *do* only have a finite amount of time, and there are, as we mentioned earlier, virtually an infinite amount of things we could be doing.

So barring that one irrational objection, this is what a prioritized life would look like. You'd be spending your time on the things that you determined mattered most to you (or the things that you inadvertently allowed to steal your time). You'd be focusing first on what mattered most. You'd be putting one task in front of another.

And as long as faith mattered most to you, and the subsequent priorities were all in precise order, and you were expending exactly the appropriate amounts of time on each one, and you were getting the results you wanted in each one—you'd be all set.

The challenge comes when you are a person who wants *more*. The struggle sets in when you want *better* for additional or all the other areas

> *The challenge comes when you are a person who wants more.*

of your life. In the scenario above, you might be feeling great about your spiritual connectedness and the time you're spending with your family, but you might not be reaching your goals at work. And you might not be okay with the struggles you are having financially.

So then, what would you do the following week? Realign your priorities, of course. You are going to redefine what is important and what is urgent.

You're going to put in more hours at the office. You're going to stay late. You're going to spend time studying. You're going to work and hustle and learn what you need to do to be more successful at the office and make more money. And you have successfully realigned your priorities, you are putting new tasks first, and by golly you are getting different results. Good for you!

And now your life looks like this:

168 HOURS/WEEK

FACULTY   FINANCES   FAITH   FAMILY   FITNESS   FUN

You created new solutions, but now you have new problems. Your reprioritization has had you working so much and spending your spare time trying to keep up with the things that really do matter to you that you haven't been to the gym in weeks. You're not so happy with how you're starting to look and your energy is starting to suffer.

Forget about having any fun or social time. You've had to let all that go in order to accomplish your objectives—which you did! And you feel better, right . . . ?

Or don't you?

Then you decide, "I'm not okay with being unhealthy! I'm going to make some changes in my life. I'm going to refocus and I'm serious that this time I'm going to get in shape!"

Not only that, but you are committed and disciplined and energized by your success at work and you are determined that "I can get in shape *and* be a top performer at the office. And

I'm not okay with not having fun because life is too short, so I'm just going to plan some more trips and travel into my schedule!"

You have made a decision to *reprioritize*. And you do it! You go to the gym, you bust your tail at work, you're still making that money and look at you making time to do the things that give you joy! And all is good . . .

Until one day you look up and your life looks like this:

168 HOURS/WEEK

FITNESS   FACULTY   FINANCES   FUN   FAMILY   FAITH

You're barely spending time with your family and you are overwhelmingly stressed and uncentered. You haven't been to church or had any reflection time for weeks.

"How can this be? I'm working harder than I've ever worked. I'm moving faster and more efficiently than I ever have. I'm doing my very best. I'm *trying* to prioritize. I'm reading all the books. I'm going to all the seminars. I have a coach. I have goals. I'm *Taking the Stairs*. I'm doing things right. I'm doing the right things and I still don't have any time!"

And just like that, you are now in the cycle that millions of us are struggling with on a daily and weekly basis. No matter how hard we try, we can't seem to get all the things that are important to us firing on all cylinders at the same time while maintaining our sanity.

We don't have peace; we have frustration.

We don't have completion; we have piles.

We don't have results; we have tasks.

Despair sets in.

And we wonder, "Is this ever going to get better? Will I ever get to a place where I have all this under control? Am I going to be working this hard forever?"

I know this is what happens, because I've been there.

But in that moment of brokenness, a thought occurs to you. "There has to be something I'm missing. There has to be another way."

There is . . .

Chapter Summary

Managing and Prioritizing Your Time

KEY POINTS

- Managing your time is one-dimensional thinking. The limitation to this strategy, however, is that there is always more to do than we can ever have time for.

- Prioritizing your time is developing the necessary ability to move one task in front of the others. While the value of this skill is more important than ever, we must realize that there is nothing about it that creates more time. It is simply borrowing time from one area of our life to focus on another to make sure the most important thing gets done first. It leaves us no strategy, though, for what to do with the remaining items that need to be completed.

UNEXPECTED FINDINGS

- There is no such thing as "time management"; there is only self-management.

- The existing constructs of time-management theory primarily offer us two solutions for creating more results in our life:

  - Doing this faster (running)

  - Perpetually reprioritizing tasks (juggling)

- This lack of strategies often results in massive stress, anxiety, frustration, despair and eventually burnout.

- "Priority Dilution" means falling victim to the "Tyranny of the Urgent," which is always pulling us away from things that we know are important but somehow don't demand our attention right now.

STARTLING STATISTICS
- Today more than 70 percent of moms are active in the workforce.

ACTION QUESTIONS
- Is it possible to do things so fast that it will eventually give me the margin in my life that I desire, or should I seek another method?

3

Multiplying Your Time

Learning to prioritize is a valuable skill, but just as managing your time has limitations, so does prioritizing your time.

I'm not saying there is anything invalid or wrong-minded about prioritizing. It is an important arrow in your quiver—a tool that you should keep sharp so it can assist you in managing your life. But it is important to realize what it *is* and what it *isn't*.

Making sure that you zero in on and complete your most important task ensures that you get it done. It enables you to control—or to largely influence—creating a singular desired result in your life. Moving certain things ahead in your queue is still a relevant and worthwhile skill. But the thing to realize is that . . .

> Prioritizing does not create more time.

Prioritizing does not create more time.

Prioritizing your time is like having the skill of blocking out one thing so that you can focus on something else. It does not give you more time than was actually there previously. It is simply a redistribution of your time.

Think about our visual of the water in the glass pitcher. When you "reprioritize" your life, you are shifting water from one glass—or area of your life—to another. But there is nothing happening that *creates* more "water." So when we prioritize, we aren't *creating* more time; we are *borrowing* time.

We are borrowing time from one area of our life to give to another. That's why the visual of the six glasses is so powerful: because it gives us a chance to *see* the dynamic that we've been able to *feel* all along—the dynamic being the disheartening pressure that results from us trying so hard to *effectively* spread our time across all the different things we have going on in our life.

This, by the way, is where the phrase "I have a lot to juggle" comes from. It is another representation of trying to keep all of these things going at once by constantly shifting resources and focus from one to the next.

It's not that there is anything wrong with juggling; there are certain times when it is a key skill to use inside of a project or season. But if juggling (reprioritizing) is your primary strategy for deciding how to use your time, then burnout is inevitable.

Why?

Because the juggling never stops! The only way juggling works successfully is to consistently and continuously *keep* juggling. And, honestly, that seems to describe a lot of our clients when we begin working with them. They just keep juggling.

In fact, I've met some of the greatest time-jugglers in the world. Not only that, but some of them have combined the efficiency paradigm of "managing time" and the effectiveness paradigm of "prioritizing time" to create . . .

An insanely fast juggler!

Meaning that, like a real juggler, they are almost *perpetually* reprioritizing what's important. The world we live in today throws so much information at us, and we can be processing so many things at once, that our priorities can literally align and then realign based on the new information in a matter of seconds.

Which, ironically, only causes us to move faster and faster and take more and more on. Because the only way we can get any additional improvements as a juggler—or with your time—is to either:

Juggle *more* balls

and/or

Juggle the ones that we have *faster.*

The *speed* element results from one-dimensional, "manage your time" efficiency thinking that tells us, "If I move learn to move faster, then I can get more in."

The *more*-balls element results from two-dimensional, "prioritize your time" effectiveness thinking that tells us, "If I learn to focus *better*—based on what is most urgent and important—then I should be able to juggle more balls."

As time goes on and we operate with those as our two primary strategies, it eventually becomes like we're sprinting on a hamster wheel *while* we're juggling 127 balls in the air. And in that case, the only way to increase our productivity when we get new inputs is to either run faster, juggle more, or both!

Which means that in a paradigm of only "managing your time" and "prioritizing your time," your only two ultimate options are to:

Go as fast as you can for as long as you can until you burn out, or

Let everything crash!

How does it feel to know that really all we are is a bunch of juggling hamsters sprinting toward an inevitable crash landing?!

Don't you feel that way sometimes? I sure do. Maybe that explains why a workplace survey that we conducted of more than four thousand people revealed that, while we are working more hours than ever before, 74 percent of us do not feel that we are maximizing our potential in professional endeavors.*

> *All we are is a bunch of juggling hamsters sprinting toward an inevitable crash landing.*

I don't know about you, but I don't like having to choose between working so hard that I burn out or being unsuccessful.

I refuse to accept those as the only two options.

Significance

Okay, then. So how *do* the most successful people think in regards to how they spend their time? What is different about the way they make their decisions compared to the rest of us juggling hamsters?

---

*Focused 40 Survey conducted by Southwestern Consulting in 2012–2013.

Well, after profiling and interviewing dozens of them, coaching hundreds of them and polling thousands of them, what we confirmed is that they really do think differently.

In *Take the Stairs*, we discovered that the most disciplined people in the world don't like discipline more than the rest of us—they only think differently about it. It turns out, the same is true about how they choose to spend their time.

While most people are still making decisions based only on the two-dimensional model of factoring in Importance and Urgency, Multipliers make a third calculation that is based on *Significance*.

Except, it's not really a *separate* calculation as much as it is an *additional* calculation. If Urgency is the x-axis, and Importance is the y-axis, then *Significance* is the z-axis. Kind of like this:

HOW LONG WILL IT MATTER?

If Urgency is "how soon does this matter?"

And Importance is "how much does this matter?"

Then Significance is "how *long* is this going to matter?"

Significance isn't a calculation that is really separate from Importance; it's the other *part* of evaluating something's Importance. This creates *three-dimensional thinking*.

A flat and flipped cross-section of the diagram above would look like this:

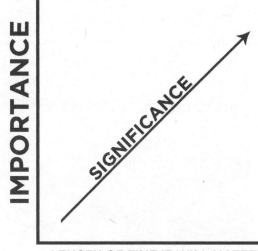

And here's why that's powerful . . .

Just like Urgency is a *part* of the Importance calculation, so is Significance. Which means that as you factor in a calculation for Significance, it begins to offset some of the weight and pull of Urgency—which is the exact cause of Priority Dilution!

Remember, Priority Dilution is allowing ourselves to be pulled out of quadrant 2 (Important but Not Urgent) always and mostly into quadrant 1 (Important and Urgent). That causes us to neglect some of the critical activities that lead to long-term success; it causes our *priorities to dilute.*

For example, let's say that you have a vision and a passion for creating better customer service, and that is an area of your business that really matters to you. Now, let's say that you have two choices on how to spend your time today:

1. Create the customer service–training program for your team.
2. Spend time providing awesome service to your customers personally.

If you *only* include the Urgency calculation, then it is obvious that you would choose option two and spend time providing awesome service personally. But if you include the Significance calculation, you realize that a great deal of consideration should be given to the idea that you create the training program.

If you manage your time and you serve customers who have *urgent* needs very *efficiently*, you could serve a lot of customers today . . . but there would be a limit.

If you prioritize your time and you serve your most *important* customers first then you would be *effective* . . . but it doesn't guarantee you'll provide exceptional service to everyone who needs it.

If you invest your time into creating the training program, however, then you make a more *significant* impact because exponentially more customers can receive great service through the influence you make on the other customer service agents.

Awesome service delivered by you to some customers is *important* and it matters today, but a program that ensures that all of your team provides awesome service to every customer is *significant* and it matters forever.

I'm not telling you that one decision is right and one is wrong. I'm not telling you that one decision is better and one decision is worse. In fact, each decision could be the "right" decision for different people in different circumstances. What I hope to convey, though, is that simply adding this one new element of consideration to your thinking instantly has an *emotional effect* on which option you choose.

Those making the Significance calculation are operating on a plane of different perspective. They are considering not only what matters *now* but also what matters *later*. Therefore that person is better able to resist the temptation of the tyranny of the urgent— which is exactly what ultra-performers do.

Here is another example. Under what circumstance would a financial advisor who deals primarily with very wealthy, more established individuals spend time today with a completely flat-broke college student?

If you measure the decision based upon what is Urgent only, the answer would be "probably under no circumstances." Because it would never make sense for that advisor to spend his time with someone who is young and broke when his time could seemingly be better spent with someone who is older and has money.

And yet when I was one of the keynote speakers at the Million Dollar Round Table, with eight thousand of the top financial advisors from more than ninety countries, I learned an important lesson from one of the top producers who was teaching a breakout session.

He said one mistake that most advisors make is that they stratify their clients based on who makes the most money. Yet they fail to account for what could happen in the future. Often their shortsightedness causes them to miss huge opportunities.

He went on, "What is going to happen to all that money when your rich client dies?" If you think for a minute, the answer becomes obvious: "They're going to pass it on to their broke kids!"

He continued, "And if you don't have a relationship with those kids when they inherit that money, what do you think they're going to do with that money? They're going to spend it! Or worse, they'll invest it with someone else. Someone they know and trust."

In that situation, spending time with the heirs wouldn't just be a nice thing to do. It would be a core priority, an income-producing activity. It would be what we at Southwestern Consulting call a "Critical Success Factor" (CSF).

Why else would a top-tier financial advisor spend time with a broke college student? What if the college student was an athlete who had a chance of going pro? Spending time with him or her right now wouldn't be critical based on Urgency alone, but when you factor in the *Significant* long-term potential, it makes more sense.

Now, these two illustrations may seem obvious to you—and they are—but this is the same way that a Multiplier would look at the choices you make about how you spend your time.

Multipliers don't just make decisions based on the here and now; they make decisions based on a perspective of how it will affect the future. It's not just a matter of additional discipline or iron will; it is a different calculation made from a different perspective.

Multiplication

Once ultra-performers realize that you can't *manage* time, and there is a limit to *borrowing* time, they intuitively learn how to *multiply* their time.

How in the world do you *multiply* your time?

Simple. And the next sentence is the singular core message of this entire book:

> *You multiply your time by spending time on things today that will give you more time tomorrow.*

You multiply your time by spending time on things today that will give you more time tomorrow.

Absent the Significance calculation, my only choice is to work faster and faster and to attempt to switch back and forth between different things. The faster I work, the more elements I can fit in, but the more I fit in, then the more things that get presented to me as urgent. Which keeps me in frenetic flux of trying to figure out how to always move faster or to take on *more*.

I spend my time every day doing that and go to bed exhausted. Then tomorrow I get up and do the same thing over again. At best, I only make marginal improvements in my results and in creating any additional "space" in my life.

But when I focus on *multiplying* my time, everything changes. My horizon is expanded and my intention shifts to beyond just today. As I start to make considerations of Significance, I start paying more attention to how spending my time today will affect tomorrow.

I realize that there are certain *investments* of my time that may *cost* me time today—sacrificing my ability to satisfy some of the Urgent temporarily—but that these investments of my time will have a positive effect on my day tomorrow by creating more margin in my life. There are things I can do today that will make tomorrow better. There are choices that I can make now that will create more space later.

That one idea alone makes me feel, for the first time in a long time, that there is a *chance* that things are about to change.

Instantly, I start to feel free.

Immediately, I have more peace.

Finally, I have a sense of hope.

I can spend my time on things today that will improve my life tomorrow.

Right away, I already know some of those things I should start doing. I should be doing *anything* that is going to make tomorrow *easier.*

And I also immediately start to know what I should stop doing! I should stop *thinking* about only today.

Suddenly it seems so obvious . . . the only way to beat the Tyranny of the Urgent is to get ahead of it and prevent it from ever happening in the first place. There is no amount of speed or efficiency or prioritization that will enable me to keep up with it on a day-to-day basis. So why even try?

> *The only way to beat the Tyranny of the Urgent is to get ahead of it and prevent it from ever happening in the first place.*

Instead, why not spend the time I have today anticipating and derailing all of the things that could become Urgent tomorrow?

For if I eliminated what was going to become Urgent tomorrow, then when I get there nothing else would be left to focus on except what is Significant—which would only perpetuate the idea that the next day there would be even less that is Urgent.

It really is that simple.

I will *multiply* my time by spending time on things today that will give me more time tomorrow.

But as is often the case, simple does not at all mean that it will be easy.

THE DRIFT

MULTIPLIER MINDSET CASE STUDY

Pete Wilson, Ministry, Cross Point Church
Nashville, Tennessee

If you think you have a lot of demands on your time, consider for a moment what life would be like if you were a pastor . . .

The primary purpose for the existence of your position is to *serve* people, and with no shortage of broken homes, broken dreams and broken hearts, you would literally have an unfortunately never-ending line of hurting people right at your door. Imagine the conflict you might feel of being available at every needy person's beck and call juxtaposed against the ceaseless pressure of making time to set the perfect example for everyone around you of what a happy family is supposed to look like.

There is no room for frustration, despair or exhaustion in your own life because—regardless of whether it's fair or if it's what you want—everyone looks at you for guidance on how a "spiritual" person should live. Keep in mind that there is no worldly incentive for any audience to pay attention to what you have to offer . . . and did I mention that the primary resource that most leaders have to motivate their team—money—is rarely, if ever, available to you?

If that were not enough, then add to it that you have to manage the expectations of people from a wide range of socio-economic backgrounds, many of whom have very strong and deep-rooted convictions about the decisions you are making and how you should be choosing to spend your time. All the while knowing that you have skeptics and critics who are waiting nearby to publicly scrutinize and quickly highlight even your smallest mistake. Running a church has many of the same challenges and pressures of running a big business. Regardless of your religious affinity, I hope you will agree that in today's society perhaps the most consistent miracle a pastor will perform is just being one.

Yet for people like Pete Wilson, dealing with these dynamics aren't pressures; they are privileges.

Pete is the senior pastor of the church that he and his wife planted, Cross Point, which in just eleven years has grown to a regular weekend attendance of more than seven thousand people. Add to that about a quarter million people following him on social media, tens of thousands of readers of his bestselling books, a group of several dozen on the church staff, three sons and a marriage to nurture, Pete unquestionably has a lot of priorities pulling on his time.

"Rory, if I'm qualified to share any ideas on how to get the most out of your time it's only because I've made as many mistakes as anyone," Pete casually offers. "For the first several years of my adult life I wrestled relentlessly with defining for myself what success looks like. Early on, I lost a lot of time because I allowed myself to define success as 'making other people happy.' It took me a long while before I finally figured out that garnering your self-worth from the approval of other people is an emotional black hole; it's like the equivalent of trying to fill up a giant lake with a little Dixie cup.

> *Garnering your self-worth from the approval of other people is an emotional black hole; it's like the equivalent of trying to fill up a giant lake with a little Dixie cup.*

"I spent my time doing what everyone else wanted me to do, and my schedule and my life was out of control. I committed the same mistake many people today do, which is that I drifted away from being significant to being busy. People who haven't determined what success is for themselves will almost always revert to being 'busy.' There is a glorification of 'busy' in our society that makes it so easy for us to confuse 'busy' with 'successful.' As human beings, we have this undeniable propensity to become obsessed with things that ultimately have little meaning in life. Social media, television, shopping and alcohol are just a few of the things that we become addicted to that ultimately have little to no significance.

"I had to get to a place where my identity wasn't gathered from the approval of other people in my life. It *had* to come from a different place or else I would constantly be feeling like a failure. And—at least for me—I couldn't just ask, 'What do I want to accomplish with my life?' but rather, I had to define success in a more significant way. Finally, I asked myself the question, 'What does God want me to accomplish with my life?' and everything changed.

"I finally set in on the idea that success for me is 'to point as many people as possible toward the hope of Christ.' What was so empowering and freeing about it was that I stopped trying to get people to like *me* and instead only focused on trying to get them to like *God*. Knowing what success looked like for me gave me clarity about exactly how I should spend my time each day. It gave me a context by which to evaluate all of my other decisions.

"Once I had that clarity, I then was able to create 'buckets' on my schedule for certain activities each week. For example, the people around me now know that while we may have forty counseling requests, I can only dedicate six hours a week to doing one-on-ones and when those slots fill up, then that is it and they have to roll forward to the next week. I might have three lunch slots set aside per week for meetings with leaders and once they are booked, they are gone. The same with one-on-one staff meetings, et cetera.

"With the backdrop of my definition of success—pointing as many people as possible toward the hope of Christ—I would be a failure if I spent forty hours per week doing all individual counseling sessions. This process created a rhythm for my life and my time that was workable and allowed me to feel good about satisfying as many demands as possible without compromising what real success looks like to me."

The scheduling process that Pete stumbled upon is very common among Multipliers and is something that we at Southwestern Consulting refer to as creating a "categorical schedule." It allows you to feel more in control by blocking a certain amount of time each day or week for *types* of activities without locking yourself into hard specifics of what might feel "rigid" and "constricting," as with traditional schedules.

As Pete conclusively points out, "This isn't just a Christian thing. No matter who you are, if you haven't defined what success means for your own life in the long term, then the higher the likelihood that things are going to feel out of control for you in the short term. Time is the one thing you can never make more of, so I don't want my life to be defined by what other people want. Most of all, I certainly don't want to allow myself to drift toward spending time on things that ultimately don't matter; when it's all said and done, I want my life to have counted for something . . . something big."

What's really driving you

It was a Saturday morning and all of our partners for South-western Consulting were in my current hometown of Nashville, Tennessee, for a visioneering retreat. "Visioneering" is a term that we borrowed from Andy Stanley, a bestselling author and founder of North Point Ministries, with outreach around the world. We love it because it represents the juxtaposition of dreaming about the future combined with engineering the plans necessary to make those dreams a reality. It's one of my favorite times of the year because now that we have grown so fast, we have partners flying in from Singapore, Australia, the United Kingdom and all over the world.

My business partner, Dustin, and I had hit the gym for an early morning workout to clear our heads and get ready for the day. Since we live only about half a mile from each other, he picked me up on the way and then we stopped at my house first on the way back.

I took a quick shower, changed and hopped back in his car so we could head to his house.

He took a quick shower and changed, and as we were walking down the hallway heading out to our meeting, something happened that changed my life forever . . .

Dustin's two-year-old baby girl—who is the sweetest little thing you've ever seen—runs down the hallway, leaps and latches her entire body around his left leg.

"Hi, Baby Haven!" Dustin says in his sweet baby voice mixed with his thick country-boy accent.

"Hi, Daddy!" she exclaims. "Where are you going?"

"Oh well, honey, Daddy has to go to work today," he replies.

And then she looks up at him with her cute curly hair, and tears immediately well up in her big brown eyes and she says, "No, Daddy! No work! Please no more work! Daddy, please! Please stay with me, Daddy, please, please!"

My heart broke instantly.

She was so sad.

Plus, I felt really bad for Dustin. What do you say to that? How do you just leave your baby behind in that moment?

Yet, it's not like you can just cancel on your partners who have literally traveled from around the world to spend this one and only day together.

And then like a bolt of lightning it hits me and something finally "clicks" in my brain clearly for the first time:

Choosing how to spend your time isn't just logical; it's emotional.

Choosing how to spend your time isn't just logical; it's emotional.

Human beings are not logical creatures. We are emotional. As human beings, we are driven by *feeling* and we are moved by *impulses*. We have a *desire* to please. We have a *yearning* to impress. We have a *need* to be accepted. We are *tempted* by pleasure. We get *tired* from work. We get *stressed* from pressure. And we are *called* to experience community and connectedness.

Oh yes.

We are definitely *emotional*.

And yet where in all of the "time-management" classes is the section that teaches you how to manage your emotions? Which book on systems strategy addresses the *human* element of our decision making? And what productivity professor has a technique for how to respond when your beautiful two-year-old girl—whom you love more than anything in the whole world—says, "Daddy, please no work!"

Where is *that*?!

Nowhere to be found, it seems; yet it is a *monumental* part of the challenge that comes with deciding how to spend our time.

And can someone explain to me how a calendar, checklist or flow chart is *really* going to help us once we're in a moment where we're already stressed, tired or tempted?

No, they can't, because it won't.

Choosing how to spend your time is no longer about better tips and tricks to manage your calendars and checklists. Those are all just more linear tools that perpetuate one-dimensional efficiency thinking to help you logically "manage your time." But "time management" is no longer logical; it's emotional.

In that split-second encounter with young Haven, everything I thought I knew had once again . . . changed. And I realized that what makes Multipliers different is not *just* their thinking; it's also how they manage their *emotions*.

It really isn't about time management; it *is* about self-management. And as I started to research and ask, study and observe exactly how it was that these people were going about spending time on things today to give themselves more time tomorrow, I discovered that the most successful people in the world have all given themselves one big thing that the rest of us have not . . .

Permission.

Specifically, they have given themselves five permissions that the rest of us have not. It is those five permissions and the frameworks they use to determine when to employ them that enable them to do what no one else can: multiply time.

Chapter Summary

Multiplying Your Time

KEY POINTS

- While most people operate and evaluate their time based on two-dimensional thinking, Multipliers consider a third factor, which is *Significance.*
- Urgent is "How soon does this matter?" Important is "How much does this matter?" and Significant is "How long does this matter?"
- You *multiply* your time by spending time on things today that give you more time (and results) tomorrow.
- The only way to avoid always dealing with urgent fires is not to deal with your fires faster, but to get out in front of them to prevent the fires from ever happening in the first place.

UNEXPECTED FINDINGS

- How we choose to spend our time is not just logical; it's emotional.
- Garnering your self-esteem and your self-worth from others will result in a never-ending route of stress and anxiety as you try to serve them without allowing you to define what success means to you.
- Multipliers regularly give themselves five emotional permissions that the rest of us do not.

STARTLING STATISTICS

- Seventy-four percent of people say they are not maximizing their potential in professional endeavors, despite working more hours than ever before.

ACTION QUESTIONS

- If you read nothing further in this book, are there things you would finally give yourself the permission to do now that you know you multiply your time by spending time on things today that give you more time tomorrow? What are they?

Part 2

The
5 Permissions

THE FOCUS FUNNEL

TASKS

PRIORITY
DILUTION

ELIMINATE

AUTOMATE

PRIORITY
CONCENTRATE

DELEGATE

PROCRASTINATE ON PURPOSE

ME

CONCENTRATE   PROCRASTINATE

NOW   **LATER**

4

Eliminate

The Permission to Ignore

My good friend Dan Miller is one of the world's most popular career coaches and the bestselling author of *48 Days to the Work You Love* and *No More Dreaded Mondays*. Dan is one of the Multipliers in my life whom I've learned a great deal from. But first and foremost, Dan is a creative.

Living about forty minutes outside of downtown Nashville in the green rolling hills of Tennessee, Dan and his wife bought a gorgeous plot of land that they lovingly refer to as The Sanctuary. It's a fitting name for the peaceful landscape of almost ten acres. People who take some of Dan's courses often get a chance to visit the location, as Dan and Joanne prefer to invite guests and clients to their home so that they can really connect with them and get to know them.

As a result, the Millers often have visitors to their property and they love giving tours. One of the highlights of the tour is an old dead tree stump in their yard. You might be wondering why anyone would care about an old dead tree stump. And in most cases they probably wouldn't. But this particular tree stump is a thing of beauty, both for how it looks and for what it has to teach us.

Several years ago, Dan was faced with a dilemma. A thundering winter storm had knocked over one of the larger cedar trees in his yard, cracking it right in the core of the tree about fourteen feet above the ground. Not only did Dan lose one of his beautiful trees, he also had this new problem, which was, what to do with the remaining stump?

Now, most people probably would've just called the tree removal service to take the stump out of the ground and haul it away. But Dan certainly isn't like most people.

After a few weeks of pondering what to do with this stump, one day he finally had an idea. He called Terry B, a lady known for her wood carvings, and explained that he had "an interesting project" for her.

Upon her arrival, Dan stated that he was just certain there was an eagle trying to get out of that damaged tree. Terry walked around it carefully for about twenty minutes and then said, "I think you're right."

Three days later she had completed her work, and where once was nothing significant, she had "uncovered" an absolutely stunning bald eagle carved at an angle into the wood allowing for a four-foot wingspan! She didn't *make* it; she *revealed* it. That eagle was there all along—she simply had to remove the buildup of time that was hiding it.

This is a real-life illustration of something that was said by French writer Antoine de Saint-Exupéry: "Perfection is achieved not when there is nothing more to add, but when there is nothing left to take away."

It is a peculiar truth about those of us who are on the journey to achieving success—we almost always focus on what we need to *add* to our lives. We look for what new strategy we need to learn that we don't already know. And we look to build on the foundation of what we already have.

> *Perfection is achieved not when there is nothing more to add, but when there is nothing left to take away.*

But what if we instead focused first on what could be *taken away* from what we're doing now? Well, that is indeed the very first practical step of becoming a Multiplier. It is asking yourself the question, "What are all of the things that I can just eliminate?"

"Eliminate" is the first of the five choices or strategies that Multipliers implement. Of the five strategies, this one has by far the widest swath of opportunity for time savings that we can immediately give ourselves tomorrow that we don't have today.

If we *multiply* our time by spending time on things today that will create more time tomorrow, then there isn't a faster way to create more margin tomorrow than by spending our time today just wiping out, deleting or removing some of the things that we're involved in that we *would be doing* tomorrow.

Just think for a moment about all of the stuff that you're doing that you don't need to be doing. And the real power here is that you are looking for things that you can just *stop* doing. No explanation. No warning. No ramp-down time. No apology. What are the things that we can just stop?

Once you try on a Multiplier's perspective and you start thinking about where you have a chance to Eliminate, you might realize that sometimes we engage in completing trivial tasks just to satisfy our need to *feel* accomplishment. Those are the first sets of activities that we can get rid of.

Honestly, have you ever completed a task that wasn't on your To Do list, and *then* added it to your To Do list afterward just so you could cross it off? We all have! Why? Because we are emotional creatures.

As a Multiplier, you are focused on results, not tasks. Success is no longer related to the *volume* of tasks you complete but rather the *Significance* of them. As Peter Drucker once said, "There is nothing so useless as doing efficiently that which should not be done at all."

Success is no longer related to the volume *of tasks you complete but rather the* Significance *of them.*

NEED TO KNOW

MULTIPLIER MINDSET CASE STUDY

Ron Lamb, Software, Reynolds and Reynolds

Dayton, Ohio

It's not every day that you stumble across someone with the pedigree of Ron Lamb. Princeton educated with an MBA from Loyola, he looks much younger than he probably is, because after twenty-three years of experience, he has become the president of a company that is *the* premier provider of software solutions for auto dealerships around the world. It just so happens to be a billion-dollar company with more than four thousand team members.

You might think that someone like that would have an insatiable egotistical urge to share his opinion on everything with everyone . . . but you couldn't be more wrong. Despite his natural charisma, Ron is one of the most humble guys you'll ever meet, and his only real concern seems to be about how he and his team can maximize their time for the benefit of their customers. In fact, a key part of his philosophy for driving productivity and customer solutions is reducing the amount of unnecessary time spent in company meetings.

"All the time I'm getting invited to meetings that I don't need to be a part of!" he begins. "We have people who are perfectly capable of making good decisions who don't need me looking over their shoulder. Our mantra is now 'Need to Know, Need to Be,' in other words who *really* needs to know the information from a meeting and who *really* needs to be there in the first place to make the decision?

"It is a blessing and a curse that Outlook allows you to invite ten to fifty people to a meeting with a couple of keystrokes. The curse is that people set meetings and go to meetings just so they can be 'in the know.' First of all, the 'need to know' is the result of emotional insecurity that we really try to eliminate from our culture. Not everyone needs to 'know' everything in order to provide a great service experience to our customers. Providing world-class software means we *need* to get code written, get code tested and get code released. We *need* to have a bias of getting stuff done; we do not *need* to have meetings just so people can be 'in the know.'

"Part of the process that we've used to help us eliminate unnecessary meetings and unnecessary attendance is a rigorous dogma to 'codify and communicate.' That means we really limit who are the 'Need to Be-ers' that truly must be in the meetings to make the decisions, and then we consistently practice reducing our decisions to concise writing that is then e-mailed out to the 'Need to Know-ers.' There may be ninety people who 'need to know' but only three people who 'need to be' [in the meeting]. So we get the three people in a room, discuss the issues, make a decision and then communicate—in written form— the decisions that were made to all of the people that really need to know. Think how much time that saves to focus on serving our customers! Not to mention the rate at which having fewer people in the room speeds up our decisions. The decision-making process slows down dramatically proportionate to the number of people in the room.

"Meetings are expensive. If you add up the value of the time of everyone in the meeting and the cost of all of the things they could be doing rather than being in the meeting, you quickly realize that unnecessary meetings must be eliminated. Some meetings are critical, but we do a regularly thorough inventory and audit of any standing meetings because you can't be out solving problems when you're trapped in a meeting.

"We've found that if you develop the practice of 'precisely codifying and effectively communicating' decisions made to the right people, that most weekly meetings can be turned into monthly meetings. If you do that, you're going to add three hours of productivity per person per month—which is as much as thirty-six hours per year per person!"

Multipliers like Ron Lamb realize that every second wasted is one second that is stolen from serving a customer or making someone else's life better. Streamlining meetings is just one example of holding every activity up to the litmus test of "does this really need to be done in the first place?"

What are all the things that you are doing that you shouldn't be doing? For most of us, there are quite a few of them. Here are just a few:

- **Re-decision:** This is reviewing a decision where we know what the right decision is and we should have already made the decision before. But because it is a difficult decision, we decided to wait on it, falsely thinking that it would be somehow easier to make the decision tomorrow than it was to make the decision today. And so now you're spending additional time reviewing something that should've already been moved on. I just eliminated half your inbox for you right there—you're welcome.
- **Watching TV:** Earlier, I mentioned the exorbitant amount of time that senior citizens spend watching TV, but the

average American over the age of two spends more than thirty-four hours a week watching TV. That means the average person will have spent nine years of their life watching television!* And that same person is coming into the office saying, "I'm too busy"? Something's wrong with this picture.

- **Unnecessary meetings:** Clients regularly tell us they have meetings every single week that are not productive. As one of our partners, Mike Weber, says, "Are you having a meeting because that is what you do every Monday at ten a.m.? Or are you having a meeting because you have an actual *reason* to have the meeting?" A survey by Salary.com reported that 47 percent of people said "meetings were their biggest waste of time at the office."

- **Long e-mails:** A long e-mail is almost a flashing sign that you need to have an in-person conversation. My wife and business partner, Amanda, has what she calls "The Preview Pane Rule," which is that if the e-mail she is reading doesn't fit entirely in her e-mail preview pane window without scrolling down, she just skips the e-mail. (It is too pane-full to read—pun intended.) She tells herself that she'll get to it later but then it could be much later. If it's longer than that preview pane, it probably warrants a phone call. By the way,

---

*David Hinckley, "Americans Spend 34 Hours a Week Watching TV, According to Nielsen Numbers," *New York Daily News*, September 19, 2012, nydailynews.com/entertainment/tv-movies/americans-spend-34-hours-week -watching-tv-nielsen-numbers-article-1.1162285.

my wife isn't alone in this; 84 percent of people ages eighteen to thirty-four use an e-mail preview pane window.*

- **Unnecessary change:** In general, I am a proponent of change but there are some people who want to change everything for the sake of making it *new*. Every change you make begets more time spent to implement that change—and we always underestimate it. Ask the question "Does it multiply your time?" If the answer is no, and things are working, then stick with what you've got.

- **Intermittent change:** Whenever you alternate between activities, time is lost. Even if you are appropriately switching between two Significant tasks at precisely the right time to do it, you lose time. To mentally disengage from one thing, then mentally and/or physically move to something else and then reengage takes time. Even if it is only microseconds between small changes, it takes time. Transitions between tasks are one of the biggest ways we lose time, and it can be a huge cost.

- **Confrontation e-mails:** Take it from me and let me save you some serious time as I am the world's leader in having done this wrong. *Never* send anything negative or even constructive about someone over e-mail. E-mail is a horrible translator of tone, and it will always cost you more time because of the damage control and relationship repair you'll have to do on the back end. Take up the issue in person.

---

*Jay Baer, "15 Email Statistics That Are Shaping the Future," Convince & Convert, convinceandconvert.com/convince-convert/15-email-statistics-that-are-shaping-the-future.

- **Doing other people's work:** Stop that! Don't step in and complete someone else's work. We'll talk about this one more later on, too . . .

- **Gossip:** The amount of hours gossip costs people and organizations getting up in each other's personal business is staggering. I subscribe to Dave Ramsey's definition of gossip, which is "complaining or talking badly about anything to anyone who can't directly do something about it." Eliminate it from your day.

- **Sharing your opinion:** I'm not sure what it is but I have such a deep emotional pull to share my opinion on *everything*. People don't need your opinion! They'll be fine on their own. Quit wasting time sharing your unsolicited feedback. Save it for the *Significant* things.

- **Unreasonable people:** Be honest, chances are you know some people whose behavior is just terrible. They are a complete drain on you. They are negative. The very sound of their name makes you cringe. Stop dealing with them! Don't tell them and don't explain why, just stop talking to them. If at all possible, just Eliminate hanging out with or doing business with people who drive you crazy. You can still "love" them, but "love them and leave them." It's not worth it.

- **Thinking about where you're going next:** One of the ways we most commonly lose time is by having to think about where we're going next. Having an ideal schedule (like we talked about in *Take the Stairs*) will take care of this one automatically. Or even beyond thinking about where you're going next, it's eliminating the *excessive* time you spend contemplating what you should do. Channel your emotion into the excellence of doing something rather than the mediocrity of deciding whether or not to do it.

- **Explanations versus experiences:** If you are a leader of any type, then here are two words that will magically *multiply* your time: *Show me*. When people have issues, ideas, challenges and circumstances, don't waste time listening to their explanations; instead, ask them to show you their experience. Not only will it reduce the time; it will reduce the drama.

> *Channel your emotion into the excellence of doing something rather than the mediocrity of deciding whether or not to do it.*

- **Unnecessary double-checking:** Don't spend a lot of time double- and triple-checking insignificant things.
- **Custom versus leveraged:** Whenever possible, eliminate the time you spend on creating custom work. In other words, try not to create things that you will never use again. Create things in a way that they can be used over and over again and incorporate into your decision making what percentage of this activity will be custom versus leveraged.
- **Over-volunteering:** Over-volunteering is a deceptive form of Priority Dilution. It appeals to both our need to feel important and our emotion to make a contribution, yet it pulls away from our already existing—and typically stacked— pile of significant priorities.

Which brings us to the first of the five fears and the *real* reason why you have a hard time Eliminating.

The word is "no"

Based on our discussions up to this point, it doesn't take a genius to figure out that next-generation self-management and *multiplying* your time is as much about deciding what not to do as it is about what to do.

But there is something that is holding you back. There is something that prevents you from incorporating this strategy. There is something inside you that makes this Eliminate idea much easier said than done.

That is this . . .

You have a tremendous fear of saying no.

In fact, in most cases you are outright terrified of uttering the actual word out loud.

"No."

You run. You hide. You whimper. You scamper. And then at the end of the day, after it all, you compromise so much of your life simply because you don't have the courage and the strength to say no.

And so what do you say? You say yes.

But it isn't a real "yes"; it's a reluctant "yes."

It's an uncommitted "yes."

It's an "I don't really want to but I guess I'm going to" yes.

And that kind of yes isn't really a yes at all. That kind of yes is really more like a "maybe."

And "maybe" is an awful place to be in life.

"Maybe" is definitely indefinite. "Maybe" is unsure. Uncertain. Uncommitted. Unexcellent.

"Maybe" keeps you stuck. "Maybe" means you are not moving toward what is in front of you and you are also not moving toward something else. "Maybe" always and only means you are moving backward.

Furthermore, allowing other people to live in "maybe" is a disservice. Your allowing them to be a "maybe" means you don't care enough about them to help them commit to a direction. It means you are condoning indecision. It means you are blessing what is mediocre.

Powerful people do not live with "maybe."

A yes is great. "Yes" is a beautiful word.

But so is no.

"No" is strong. "No" is clear. "No" is resolute.

"No" allows others to move on with their lives. And beyond that, "no" helps bring another person closer to a real yes.

But "maybe" is unacceptable.

You aren't helping anyone by being a reluctant yes.

A reluctant yes is more of a disservice than a favor.

A reluctant yes is more of a disservice than a favor.

A powerful person knows that there is emotional energy tied up in any unmade decision. A Multiplier knows that you can't accomplish greatness with "kind of," "sort of" or "maybe."

Let your yes be yes and your no be no.

Quit living in maybe.

"But, Rory, saying no is so hard!"

"No, it is not. Say it with me."

"No."

"C'mon, say it with me. Right now, out loud."

"No."

"Say it. Let me hear you."

"No."

"Say it proudly!"

"No."

"Say it at me, I don't care."

"No."

"Doesn't that feel good? Say it again."

"No."

"Good for you! Look, you did it."

Actually, contrary to what you might think about yourself, you've been saying no all along.

You might think that you are a "people pleaser." You might believe that you are a kind and willing steward always available to serve the needs of everyone else. You might even take pride in the fact that in all your life, you've never said no.

But you are wrong.

Let me clue you in on something that took me a long, painful time to learn.

You are always saying no to something. Any time you say yes to one thing, you are simultaneously saying no to something else.

You are *always* saying no to something. Any time you say yes to one thing, you are simultaneously saying no to something else.

You *cannot* say yes without also implicitly saying no.

By saying yes to reading this book right now, you are quietly saying no to an infinite number of other things you could be doing.

When you say yes to volunteering for that position that you don't really want to take, you are quietly saying no to the fitness goals you set for yourself.

To a Multiplier, the question is, "Am I saying yes to the things that create more time tomorrow, and am I saying no to the things that don't?"

Having context and consideration for what you are quietly saying no to does help tremendously in being able to actually turn down a person or an opportunity that you are presented with. Because we are creatures of emotion, however, it still can be rather difficult.

But there is more good news that will help . . .

On February 15, 2006, at 4:45 in the afternoon, I wrote an e-mail to one very famous author. I caught wind that he was not too far from the area where I was and so I requested a meeting with him. I knew it was a long shot, but I figured, *What the heck!*

On February 17, 2006, at 5:52 in the evening, I received my first rejection. It was not from the author personally but from a person in their office. The thing that shocked me was not only did they respond to me, but responded rather quickly and pleasantly. I received two paragraphs with useful information, a redirection to additional resources, and it included uplifting language such "Thank you so much for your e-mail, which I have shared with _____." And "although meeting with you at this time will unfortunately not be an option, _____ truly appreciates you taking the time to write, and deeply wishes you all the best."

Well of course, I had to respond to that, so on February 18, 2006, at 12:27 p.m., I replied, thanking them for such a thoughtful and articulate response. This time I offered to come work for them—for free!

On Saturday, March 11, 2006, at 2:10 p.m., the author responded to me personally. I thought *surely* I was in! It was, however, another rejection. But this time it was personal. It made me feel really good that the author actually took the time to address me directly. And yet again the language was so encouraging and uplifting.

Here is some of what it said: "Thank you for your e-mail and kind words . . . I sincerely appreciate your invitation to meet. Right now, I've promised [my spouse] that I will not add any discretionary get-togethers to my local schedule. My calendar has become so tight that I need to protect the increasingly limited time I have at home for family time. . . . I hope you can understand my need to do this." Then once again I was directed toward helpful resources, and the letter closed with "I truly wish you all the best."

I let it rest for a while.

Then in May 2008, I happened to be back in the same area and thought that enough time had passed that it would be good to approach this author again. And I thought perhaps they would be impressed that I had kept such detailed records of our initial encounters that when I requested another in-person meeting, I copied the entire original set of e-mail strings all into the same e-mail—and one week later I got another response.

This time it was from a different person in the office. And this time . . .

Well, I was rejected again! The e-mail said, "_____ is truly appreciative of all of your support and is encouraged by your consistent desire to meet. At this time, it is not a possibility because _____ is tied up in intensive research and writing of the next book. We hope and trust that your career is progressing along nicely and do keep us up to date!" At which point I thought to myself, *Wow, these people sure know how to make a guy feel good—and still lay down a rejection!*

On July 28, 2011, I had a surefire plan. I had just finished the manuscript for *Take the Stairs* for the deal I had secured with a major New York publisher. I was certain the author would appreciate not only that I was becoming a real author, and not only that I *still* had our entire correspondence history, but they would be honored that I asked for an author endorsement.

So I sent an advance copy of *Take the Stairs*, along with our entire communication history and a short update of all I had been up to—and a request for a quick endorsement.

On August 18, 2011, I got a physical letter with a handwritten signature in the mail. It said:

Dear Rory,

Congratulations on writing your first book. I'm flattered that you would ask me to write an endorsement.

Rory, my practice on endorsements that I require of myself is that I become thoroughly acquainted with the ideas or that I personally know the author before deciding whether to endorse. This allows my endorsement to really *be* an endorsement, and enables me to make a thoughtful and credible comment, in the event that I do decide to endorse.

Given the backlog of commitments already on my plate, I'm afraid I lack the bandwidth to add another piece to the stack clamoring for my attention.

Having been through the adventure of writing, I fully appreciate the exhilaration, exhaustion and anxiety of publishing a book. I extend to you my warmest and best wishes for great success with Take the Stairs, *and I hope you can understand.*

Yours sincerely,

_____

Man, I got told no and I loved it! Handwritten, custom-tailored, on thick letter stock . . . it was the best rejection ever!

Fast forward a little further . . .

On October 4, 2012, I was speaking in the very city where the author lives. At this point I was now a *New York Times* bestselling author.

_____ has a copy of our entire e-mail communication, they've sent me a handwritten letter, they have a copy of my book, and we were on the same bestseller list at the same time! This author now *knows* who I am; I'm sure of it.

After all these years, I am finally going to get a chance to meet this person. I send a note laying out two options. The first is to come watch me speak. The second is for me to come meet them anywhere they would like for just thirty minutes.

What happened?

I did not get to meet the author. But I also did not get a rejection letter, either.

This delightful young woman approaches me after my speech

and says, "Rory, it's really great to meet you. Unfortunately _____ could not come but did want me to stop by and send regards. _____ has read *Take the Stairs* and was rather impressed by it. Our entire office wishes you all the very best!"

This time, the author sent someone *from* their office *physically* to where I was speaking to turn me down . . . *in person*!

What does this entire story prove?

Other than I'm incredibly persistent and that this person *really* doesn't want to meet with me, it proves this: You can say no and still be nice!

You can say no and still be nice!

This author has been rejecting me *for seven years*. Not to mention that it's been via multiple media! And I love it. I'm more endeared to them than I ever have been before because of the *way* they are telling me no.

They are telling me no with honesty. They are telling me no with integrity. They are telling me no with class. And they are clearly telling me *no*.

They aren't misleading me. They aren't lying to me. They aren't making me wrong. They aren't getting mad or annoyed at me. And that makes me feel like they aren't really rejecting *me*; they just don't have time to meet.

And I'm fine with that. I can appreciate that. Heck, I'm taking lessons from it!

Now that I'm an author and a husband, I can relate to not having availability for "discretionary get-togethers" and strangers wanting your endorsement and time.

Guess what?

So can all the people you know!

People can take no. But they want to be treated with dignity. They want to be treated honestly. And they want to be treated carefully.

So, tell them no. And if you are a big giant softie who is afraid of upsetting people, then make it the biggest, best-est, nicest, classiest no they've ever gotten!

And if you have a hard time saying the actual word "no," here are some honest, straightforward phrases to help you deliver the bad news:

As much as I would like to help you, I simply can't right now . . .

I'm sorry, I just much prefer not to . . .

I'm afraid I simply lack the bandwidth right now to commit to doing this . . .

Unfortunately, it's not in my best interest to take this on at the moment . . .

I'm really stretched thin right now and I promised myself I wouldn't take on anything else . . .

To be honest, this is just something I really don't want to do . . .

The first permission

I hope you now feel empowered to say no—and that you understand the *Significance* of saying it.

But the reality is that you're not going to be able to fully execute the Eliminate strategy until you take the next step.

And that is, you have to give yourself the *permission* to Ignore.

It's fine to be nice and it's good to be respectful, but for you to gain peace and perspective in your life, you have to learn to be okay with just *Ignoring* certain things.

You need to free yourself of the need to feel like you have to be everything to everyone.

You have to let go of the absurd idea that you owe everyone an explanation.

You have to rewrite the story that you have to take on everything that comes your way.

You have to learn to just flat out Ignore certain things.

Delete it. Eliminate it. Eradicate it. Get rid of it.

If the only reason you are doing something is because you feel guilty about *not* doing it—then don't do it.

If the only reason you are doing something is because you have a fear of what you might miss out on—don't do it.

If the only reason you are doing something is because you feel obligated just because someone asked you to do it—don't do it.

To be a Multiplier, you have to constantly be asking yourself, "Is this task something I can live without? Does it multiply my time? Does what I'm doing right now create more time tomorrow—or less?"

The permission to Ignore is the first of the five permissions in the Focus Funnel, and it corresponds with the first of the five choices for *Multiplying Your Time*, which is to Eliminate.

THE FOCUS FUNNEL

5 PERMISSIONS   TASKS   5 CHOICES

IGNORE   ELIMINATE

ME

You are either consciously saying no to the things that don't matter, or you are unconsciously saying no to the things that do.

So figure out which activities you want to do and which ones create more time, results or satisfaction tomorrow, and say yes to those and no to the others.

You are either consciously saying no to the things that don't matter, or you are unconsciously saying no to the things that do.

Anytime you say yes to one thing, you are simultaneously saying no to something else.

Realize that when you say yes to . . .

- Watching TV . . .
- Giving in to your call reluctance . . .
- Succumbing to procrastination . . .

- Your fear . . .
- Wasting time . . .

You just said no to . . .

- More time with your kids
- More time with your spouse
- Reaching your financial goals
- Achieving your dreams

You just said no to *multiplying* your time.

Sometimes people ask me, "Rory, why do you work so intensely every minute of every day when you are at work or on an airplane?" It's because the way I look at it, every second that I don't is one more second that I'm stealing from my family.

And I won't steal from my family just so I can be *comfortable.*

Instead, I give myself permission to Ignore, and I will learn to say no to the things that don't matter so that I can say yes to the things that do.

Chapter Summary

Eliminate: The Permission to Ignore

KEY POINTS

- "Perfection is achieved not when there is nothing more to add, but when there is nothing left to take away."
- The most immediate area of improvement in multiplying our time is taking inventory of all the things we can simply stop doing.
- Most of us have a deep-rooted fear of saying no.
- Give yourself the permission to Ignore without ramping down time or needing to explain anything to anyone. Just Eliminate it!

UNEXPECTED FINDINGS

- You are always saying no to something. You are either consciously saying no to the things that don't matter or you are unconsciously saying no to the things that do.
- You aren't doing anyone any favors by saying yes to something that you really want to say no to.
- You can say no and still be nice.

STARTLING STATISTICS

- The average person will spend nine years of his or her life watching television.

ACTION QUESTIONS

- What are you currently saying yes to that is causing you to say no to your goals or your family?

5

Automate

The Permission to Invest

One of the wealthier people I know was sitting with me outside a coffee shop in southern California when I asked him this question:

"What do you think the primary difference is between rich people who acquire lots of money and everyone else?"

His response . . .

"Well, Rory, think of it this way, if you were to go into this coffee shop to order a coffee and you could hear the way that people were thinking about the decision, you'd likely hear at least three completely different ways of thinking . . ."

The first group—the people least likely to grow wealthy over time—would ask themselves two questions. The first question is "Do I want this five-dollar coffee?" And assuming the answer is yes, the second question is "What do I have to do to get myself this coffee?" They might beg for it, borrow money from a friend or even buy it on credit. Governed by impulses, they'd do just about *anything* to get the coffee.

The second group—the people most likely to end up comfortable but not wealthy—would ask themselves two questions: "Do I want this five-dollar coffee?" And assuming the answer is yes, the second question is, "Do I have five dollars?" That seems like a perfectly reasonable line of thinking—and it is. In fact, that is how *most* people think; which is exactly what makes most people *average* or *middle class*.

The third group—the people most likely to be rich over time—would ask themselves two questions: "Do I want this five-dollar coffee?" Assuming the answer is yes, however, their second question is much different from the first two groups.

Their next thought is, "If I spend five dollars on this coffee, then that is five dollars I will not be spending on something else." That is five dollars they won't be investing in the stock market, or real estate, or a business, or in themselves. Specifically, they realize that is five dollars they won't be *investing*.

A wealthy person familiar with compounding interest knows that five dollars invested today at an 8 percent interest rate for thirty years would be worth about fifty dollars.*

So their question is not: "What do I have to do to get this coffee?"

And their question is not: "Do I have five dollars?"

Instead, their question is: "Is this five-dollar coffee worth fifty dollars to me thirty years from now?"

---

*U.S. Securities and Exchange Commission, "Compound Interest Calculator," investor.gov/tools/calculators/compound-interest-calculator#.UxiOj15sieB.

Now, the tricky part is that they might still choose to get the coffee. That is why you can't look externally at one single financial decision someone makes and determine if she or he is on track to amass great wealth.

You can, however, likely determine if someone will one day be rich by following their *thought process* on how they make one financial decision.

Editor of *Success* magazine, author of *The Compound Effect* and good friend Darren Hardy is the person who shared the story above with me.

And for me, growing up in a trailer park and apartments, raised most of my young life by a single mom, this line of thinking was an absolute shock. It was a completely different way of thinking than anything I had ever been exposed to.

Notice that there are two things happening in this story:

1. The first is a calculation of *opportunity cost*. In other words, it is realizing that if I spend five dollars on this coffee, it is five dollars that I'm not spending on a business, an investment or in personal development (which, by the way, is something that many wealthy people take very seriously and invest a lot of time and money in). By simply realizing that one purchase will simultaneously *cancel out* an *opportunity* to invest somewhere else, you will find the emotional temptation of the decision at hand almost instantly reduced. This is the power of considering *opportunity cost*.
2. The second is a calculation I'm going to call *hidden cost*. To me, hidden cost is the extrapolation of potential additional benefits or costs associated with a certain *opportunity cost*.

In this example, the opportunity cost is the five dollars not invested; but the *hidden cost* is the potential additional forty-five dollars that would be gained in interest by choosing to spend that five dollars in another way. When you calculate this decision, you can begin to realize that a simple five-dollar coffee doesn't just cost five dollars. Instead, it costs you five dollars *actual cost* plus five dollars of *opportunity cost* plus forty-five dollars of *hidden cost*, for a total of fifty-five dollars!

Would you pay fifty-five dollars for a coffee? Probably not. I'm not telling you to never drink coffee again, but I am telling you that you should be acutely aware of how much *every single dollar spent* affects your future wealth.

It's not just coffee; it's any regularly occurring expense.

If you are a smoker, then you may want to know that according to the American Lung Association, the average cost of a pack of cigarettes is $5.51, of which $1.47 is just taxes.[*] And the average smoker spends fifteen hundred dollars a year on cigarettes.[†] If you were planning on smoking from the time you were twenty until you reached age sixty, then perhaps you are curious to know how much fifteen hundred dollars invested every year for forty years at 8 percent is worth?

---

[*]American Lung Association, "The United States Facts," lung.org/stop-smoking/tobacco-control-advocacy/reports-resources/cessation-economic-benefits/states/united-states.html.

[†]Loren Berlin, "Do Smokers Know How Much They Spend on Cigarettes?" *Daily Finance*, June 22, 2011, dailyfinance.com/2011/06/22/do-smokers-know-how-they-much-spend-on-cigarettes.

A whopping $421,172.56.

Now, you might be thinking, "Rory, this is a crazy exaggeration," but I promise you it is not; it is simple math. Calculating these very *real* hidden costs is something I like to call "Multiplier's Math."

And it is one of the key differences in how wealthy people think compared to everyone else. It's one of the reasons they are wealthy and others are not. It is one of the reasons why they don't fall victim to their initial emotional impulses and so many of us do.

As I've said, it's not *just* in the choices that someone makes; but rather in *the thinking* that leads to those choices.

Time is money. Or is it?

The concept of "hidden cost" teaches us anything that wastes your time is a waste of your money. We've all heard the cliché that "time is money." And most of us *sort of* understand it.

Anything that wastes your time is a waste of your money.

Because many of us have been paid hourly at some point in our lives, we *get* the idea that if I don't spend my time working today then I don't get paid my money. But to a Multiplier, there is much more to it than that.

Multipliers, who live in a world of evaluating everything based on Significance—how long this decision is going to matter—are constantly thinking longer term. It's almost as if they are making a perpetual account for compounding interest.

It's like they have their own secret school subject that no one else knows about: Multiplier's Math.

Money is a good illustration of the dynamic because it makes this idea of Significance tangible.

Think of your money as if it were your army. Every dollar that you spend is like losing one member of your troops. Every dollar that you save or invest, however, grows your army.

Why? Because of exactly what we said above: compounding interest.

Compounding interest occurs when your investment earns interest on the previous interest that has been acquired. So, if I invested ten dollars at a 10 percent annual interest rate (or rate of return), then the first year I would earn one dollar in interest.

The magic happens in year two though, because I would earn 10 percent on eleven dollars, not ten!

So in year two, I would make $1.10 in interest (eleven dollars times 10 percent) rather than just one dollar.

And my total net worth at that point would be $12.10 when I originally started with only ten dollars.

My army is multiplying itself; my net worth is growing without my doing anything.

Another way of thinking about it is that I'm getting paid to wait on spending my money. My money works hard for me to make more and more money.

The example above with ten dollars might not seem all that compelling, but even ten dollars invested at 10 percent for forty years would be worth $452! So your army acquired and developed 442 more soldiers for you over forty years!

Change the initial ten-dollar investment to a twenty-five-thousand-dollar investment, keeping a 10 percent rate of return, and your army grows to $1,131,481 forty years from now!

If you knew you could become a millionaire by sacrificing, squeezing, tightening, working, pushing and disciplining yourself to save twenty-five thousand dollars while you were young, would you do it? Would you give up the new car, new TV, new furniture or new house for a couple of years now so that you could be a virtually guaranteed *millionaire* later?

That is exactly how it is, but no one is reminding you of this on a daily basis. You have to be the person reminding yourself. And you need to surround yourself with people, coaches and resources that remind you of the incredible power of compounding interest and Significance thinking.

By the way, one of the quickest ways to do rough math of compounding interest in your head is to use the "Rule of 72." The Rule of 72 says that if you divide the rate of return (interest rate) you are getting into 72, that will tell you approximately how many years it will take to double any amount of money at that interest rate.

For example, if you have a 10 percent annual interest rate, then it will take 7.2 years for you to double your money (72/10) no matter what amount of money you have invested; and that amount will double again every 7.2 years. If you get an 8 percent interest rate, then it will take nine years for you to double your money (72/8). If you get a 6 percent interest rate, then it will take twelve years for you to double your money (72/6) or for your "army to double itself."

If you are investing money, you are making money and multiplying your army.

If you are spending money, you are losing money and depleting your army.

If you are borrowing money, you are using your money to build someone else's army.

Wealthy people and Multipliers understand the power of compounding interest and that the most powerful money-making tool on the planet is not a get-rich-quick scheme but simply saving and investing as much money as fast and as early as possible in your life.

So, do you get the big idea here?

Time is *not* money. Time is worth way more than money.

Time is not *money. Time is worth way more than money.*

I don't *just* mean that "time is worth more than money" in the altruistic, spiritual or profound sense.

I mean that time is *literally* and *mathematically* worth more than money. Not only because time is a scarce and finite resource and money isn't. And not just because time is the one thing you can never get back. But because when used right, time makes money into more money!

There is no easier way to make more money than compounding interest. No employee, team member or other resource has ever worked harder than compounding interest. Compounding interest relentlessly works twenty-four hours a day, seven days a week to multiply your army and make you more money—without your doing anything!

The second permission

So what does all this money talk have to do with automation? I'm glad you asked. It has to do with your fear.

Just like you know you should Eliminate but you have a fear of saying no, you know you should Automate but you have a fear of not being able to afford it.

You know you need that new piece of technology, but you're still debating whether or not it's worth it.

You know you need to spend some time improving the systems you use around the office, but you're still convincing yourself that you don't have the time.

How much time do you spend doing the same things again and again?

How many times have you thought, "What we really should do is invest a little money into making this better"?

How often are you reentering the same data over and over?

How many things are you doing that are completely regimented and routine, yet you are spending your precious time doing something that a simple computer program could do?

There are things all around your life and your business that should be automated. They should be improved. They should be streamlined.

And yet it doesn't matter if we're working with a Fortune 100 executive or we're coaching a financial advisor one-on-one, they all say the same exact thing . . .

"I just don't think we have the time or the money to afford this right now."

They are missing the second permission of multiplying your time. You need to give yourself the permission to Invest.

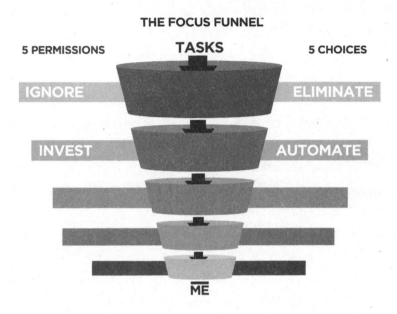

If there is a system that you know you need, that you know will save you massive amounts of time, then you can't afford *not* to implement it!

Every moment that passes that you don't Automate something that could be, you are exponentially losing future time.

The negative impact of waiting to invest your money is the exact same negative impact of waiting to invest into something that can be Automated to save you time.

The key insight from all of these investment principles is to realize that automation is to your time what compounding interest is to your money.

Yes, you will be trading time and money that you would have today. But it is going to *multiply* to-morrow. And the next day. And the next day. And then that number is going to be *multiplied* by the entire number of people who are using the system.

> *Automation is to your time what compounding interest is to your money.*

Automation can be made to work for you twenty-four hours a day, seven days a week to save you time and time again.

- The money that companies invest with us to restructure their sales and recruiting systems is literally fractions of pennies compared to the multiplying effect it will have on their increased revenue, reduced procrastination and improved employee retention over all the coming years.
- Those who invest money into a coach who can help them create better systems and automation are going to make their money back many times over, just as if they put that money into a mutual fund.
- A huge company with thousands of employees spending millions of dollars on a new system that actually works and saves everyone time will likely make billions in return.

One thing that is always more expensive than a good system is not having a system at all.

And each moment that you don't *do the things you know you should be doing*, you are stealing from your future self.

It's one more reason procrastination is the most expensive invisible cost in business today.

INVEST WHERE YOU CAN G.R.O.W.

MULTIPLIER MINDSET CASE STUDY

Scott Bormann, Pharmaceuticals

Kansas City, Kansas

If there is one industry that is challenging and competitive, it's pharmaceuticals. Think about the amount of time and money that goes into all the research that can take place *years* before ever even finding a unique and marketable drug. And consider the wide array of sophisticated competitors who are investing tens of millions of dollars vying for the very same customer dollars. The risks are high, the bets are big, and time and money are of the essence because if you are late to the party, then you might as well not even show up.

In spite of these incredibly rigorous pressures, Scott Bormann, an executive for one of the world's most recognizable global animal health companies, seems rather relaxed as we talk through some of the strategy behind one of the company's biggest launches in years. In addition to overseeing more than five hundred people in North America, Scott also is one of a handful of key decision makers responsible for coordinating a global launch and rollout of a new companion animal product—a large part of which will include Scott and his team working to persuade thousands of very intelligent and budget-conscious veterinarians as to the benefits of the new product and why it's worth a potential adjustment in their business model to try it out.

Diving right in, I hit him with the question "What is the biggest challenge you have in relation to your time today?" Casually mild-mannered yet incredibly intense, he responds without even taking a breath, "That's an easy one. It is prioritizing our key impact areas. In other words, it's constantly working to answer the question 'What can I do right now that will have the greatest impact on our business and for our customers?' It is looking ahead to the future to determine where does it make sense for us to invest now so that we can benefit from exponential growth tomorrow."

"Sure, but how do you go about calculating that?" I challenge.

"That is quite an important question, actually," he affirms. "It is one of the critical functions of a leader and one that many struggle with. Most of us either see good opportunities and don't take action because we are unsure, or we invest into every new possible thing that comes our way. Both are losing strategies. One simple technique that has helped me navigate the appropriate dichotomy of those two dynamics to determine which investments make sense and which ones don't is using something I call G.R.O.W.

"The overarching theme is analyzing whether or not the opportunity in front of us really sets the foundation to allow us to G.R.O.W. if we properly execute it. But each letter accounts for a different part of the consideration.

For example, the 'G' stands for 'Goal Alignment.' If we make this investment or change, will the resulting impact be in alignment with what we want our future goals to be? There are all kinds of things that we *could* be investing in, but the first step in knowing whether or not we *should* is by evaluating if the positive outcomes would actually put us where we are saying we want to go. You'd be amazed at how many teams and people pass on things that would take them precisely to where they want to be because they are afraid of a little investment. And inversely, how many engage in ideas just because they have them, only to find out later that even the ultimate 'successful' completion of those projects have taken them off course.

"Once we establish that choosing something could potentially move us down the right path, then the 'R' stands for 'Realistic Possibility.' Is there an infrastructure that allows you to accomplish that objective? The answer may be no and so that leaves you with another question: 'If not, then as a leader, what do I have to do to create it, or should I abandon it altogether?' This is often where you have to invest in getting some good data to help you understand the reality of the market and of your own strengths and weaknesses.

"It may also mean investing time into retraining, reorganizing, restructuring, reprioritizing, reallocating resources, removing people or repositioning people. As a practical example, when we decided to bring this new product to market, we not only had to invest all of the money into the development of the product, but we also had to invest time into restructuring our teams and geo-graphic responsibilities in order to make us more nimble in servicing our customers' needs. It was painful but neces-sary.

"If evaluating 'R'—'Realistic Possibility'—is essentially an assessment of your own internal strengths and weak-nesses, then 'O'—'Opportunity Value'—is an assessment of the potential external value of taking this chance and mak-ing this investment. Can you really see yourself competing in that space? And again, it is often rooted in data-driven research which helps you make sure that the size of the market you're entering into, the scope of the project, the frequency of the sale, and the revenue and expenses all make sense and pay off for you in the long haul. You can't just decide it's a good idea for today, you have to think about what the likely Opportunity Value is and where the real growth will come from in the long term.

"If the first three of these items in the G.R.O.W. acronym are in affirmative alignment, then we had better optimize and invest in the opportunity to take advantage! The last consideration is to simply figure out what is the 'W'—'Way Forward.' At that point it is simply a matter of determining how we get there and at what rate we can get it done. This is the game plan. It's the marching orders. It's the go-to market strategy. It's pulling the trigger. As you would say, it's when it's time to minimize minutiae and *Take the Stairs*!"

After Scott and I were done talking, I got the sense that he, like most Multipliers, goes through a simple common-sense checklist like this (that really is not so common), and if an opportunity meets the criteria, then they feel confident making the investment and they make the decision to move forward. But most of us don't. Most of us know what we should do, but we hesitate. While it is prudent to take a moment to breathe and consider the impacts of our choices, if we wait too long, we miss out on the opportunity—and that can be a great cost. Or as Scott emphatically punctuated our conversation, "If we end up doing something wrong, we can always correct it, but if we just sit around and pontificate and procrastinate, then there isn't anything we can do with it. Therefore, the greatest sin isn't doing the *wrong* thing; it's doing *nothing*."

> *The greatest sin isn't doing the* wrong *thing; it's doing* nothing.

There is a very broad range of things that you can automate today so that you won't have to manually complete them tomorrow. It applies to million-dollar investments at big corporations that save thousands of hours over a year, and it applies to homemakers spending a little bit of time to set up a new system that will save them a few minutes every month. Either way, it is powerful and worthwhile because of this dynamic of *compounding time*.

Some are specifics and some are concepts, but here are a few practical examples of automation:

- **Frequently asked questions (FAQs):** A simple idea that any small business or big business can do is to invest some time into an easy-to-use, easy-to-find, well-thought-out list of answers to FAQs. Seen as a nuisance of little value to some companies, this can be a tremendously valuable tool for customers that not only satisfies them but also saves you the time of having to handle the same questions over and over and over again.

- **Disorganized re-creation:** It baffles me how much time is spent in many organizations—even some of our large, notable consulting clients—re-creating things that already exist. This happens because there is no system for effective knowledge transfer and no effective method of searching and data sharing.

- **Online bill pay:** Spend a couple hours setting up all of your regular monthly bills to be paid automatically through bank draft. This saves you the time, energy and stress of having to keep up with the bills each month. Do the same thing with your investments by automatically depositing money out of your paycheck each month.

- **Data backup sync:** This is one that you won't wish you did until it's too late. A person calculating only with Urgency says, "I don't have time to stop and do anything," but someone considering Significance says, "The one thing I always have time for is to back up my data." You don't want to learn this the hard way. Invest some time and set it up; usually it can even be Automated.

- **NeatReceipts:** One of the best investments I've ever made, this little machine allows you to stuff piles of receipts, paper and business cards into it and scan them in a matter of seconds. You've probably seen the infomercials for it and thought it was a gimmick, but it's not. It can literally eliminate storing any kind of papers or receipts.

- **Social media management:** If you're not already, you should be using a tool like Hootsuite or SocialOomph that allows you to schedule tweets, blog posts, Facebook updates and so on, to multiple online locations, all from one central dashboard. It allows you to be "present" in online communities without having to *actually* be there all day. This is the virtual mechanism for being able to be in two places at once *and* travel into the future!

- **Past client follow-up:** A common consulting project for us as of late has been helping companies craft an ongoing customer appreciation strategy. It is an automated way, using a variety of different media, to stay in regular contact with your past clients (or prospects) just to show them that you care. Repeat business is almost always more profitable than new business.

- **Online learning:** With the emergence of online learning platforms like Schoox (schoox.com), you can create training videos *once* today on everything someone on your team needs to know to be successful. After that, you will be able to host the videos in an online learning management system (LMS), to which you can then send your trainees to take your own online courses. You can track their progress, test for comprehension and even access other online courses from outside content providers. Our entire Southwestern Consulting online academy for both internal training of our own team and our public video training courses are hosted on Schoox—which combines online learning with social media–type tools for engagement you can't get in a trad-itional LMS. We have courses on a variety of different topics, such as sales training, leadership, presentation skills, personal finance, conflict resolution, social media and productivity—both for our own team and for clients and prospects. We've even begun helping companies lay out a content management strategy for how they can reduce training costs in time and money by organizing and hosting their own online academies.

- **Talk tracks:** Similar to having FAQs, empower your team with a set of talk tracks to handle difficult or recurring situ-ations. Whether they are in sales, customer service, collec-tions or general services, you can improve the quality and consistency of the service that you provide while simultane-ously reducing the amount of questions that come to you. Developing talk tracks for sales teams and recruiters is one of the primary reasons companies engage Southwestern Consulting for sales training.

- **Drop shipping:** This is another one of the beauties of the modern day world. There are thousands of vendors to whom you can outsource your customer fulfillment and shipping. Sale happens, product is delivered; you do nothing.

We can also zoom out to a broader discussion of where and how Automate applies to all of us: Any time you can set up a system whereby someone can reduce the amount of "think time" she has to spend to complete a regimented task, you will have cre-ated savings.

So it's not necessarily about technology—although this is one of the core benefit areas of technology.

- A stay-at-home mom or dad can eliminate "think time" and/or arguments about whose turn it is to take out the trash simply by creating an agreed-upon chore chart.
- Salespeople can reduce the amount of "think time" or call reluctance they might experience by scheduling every follow-up call they need to make on any given day, and not just the ones that are at mutually agreed-upon set times. In our coaching program we've found that a salesperson's fear reduces dramatically when he or she knows who are the first five call prospects for the following day.
- CEOs can eliminate the "think time" or back-and-forth e-mails that they might have with an assistant about times they are available by investing the time to create what we mentioned in the Pete Wilson profile as a *categorical schedule*. Unlike a traditional schedule where you might schedule specific appointments or tasks at specific times, a categorical schedule is one where you schedule blocks of allotted time for certain *types* of activities to occur. Categorical schedules take the "think time" out of making sure you are spending the right amount of time on the right types of activities in any given week.
- A project manager can reduce "think time" and feeling overwhelmed by the size of his inbox by setting up e-mail rules so that certain types of e-mails automatically flow into a separate folder.

The power is not in any *one* of these ideas, as these are just a handful of fairly universal examples. The power is not *necessarily* in finding new apps or existing tools like these or others that will show up in the future.

The power is in understanding the thinking and the magnitude of the Automate principle. And in opening your eyes to everything that repeats over and over again in your business, to see how much of it can be automated.

Multiple system chaos no more

When we first started Southwestern Consulting, the few people we had on our team had to do everything. I personally was one of the salespeople. I was an executive, I was the janitor, I was the IT guy, I was the marketing department and so on. Anyone who has ever been in a small business can undoubtedly relate.

We had big dreams. Our mission was to help people achieve their goals in life and to become the best and most recognizable sales training company in the world.

One of the things I love about small business owners is that their success completely depends on them. They have to work. They have no other choice. And that is what we did: We worked!

In 2006, when it all began, we basically had no money. We couldn't afford office space, we couldn't afford any technology and we couldn't buy leads. I remember sitting by the community pool at the Oak Woods apartment complex in Santa Clara, California, with my other three partners as we took a Yellow Pages phone book and ripped it into fourths. We each took a stack and said, "You call these people, I'll call those."

We made hundreds of dials every day. We cold-called companies and offered them a free custom-tailored one-hour sales training session for their team. The deal was that we would spend the time teaming up with the sales manager to determine what their team really needed. Then, we'd put the work into creating the training session. And finally we'd dedicate our time, free of charge, to come in and deliver a first-rate group training presentation. Assuming we did a terrific job, the only thing we asked for in return was the chance to introduce some of our coaching and consulting services to the team. (It's the same model that our now more than seventy consultants still follow today as a way of introducing ourselves and earning trust.)

Since we were bootstrapping the company, we were selling all day long, and then we didn't actually *build* the business until nights and weekends. I remember waking up at six a.m. and literally working from seven a.m. till midnight, Monday through Saturday for the first two years. Having worked eighty hours a week in the Southwestern Advantage summer program when I was in college, I was already used to working long hours.

The challenge here was that we were doing *everything*. And it required so many different skill sets just to stay afloat, yet we didn't have any money to pay a lot of people to help us. It was incredible how much data had to be transferred back and forth about who bought, who scheduled, who sold, who paid, who didn't pay, what needed to be sent out and so on. There was no way to see what conversations we were each having with prospects and customers.

We were entering data everywhere. We had hundreds of different spreadsheets that were creating thousands of e-mails back and forth among us—that none of us had time to respond to. And our most prized asset, our customers, were nearly impossible to keep up with because some of them were on spreadsheets, some were in stacks of business cards, some were in the computer and some were on sticky notes.

Over time, the most frustrating part was how hard we were working and yet how difficult it was to stay in touch with our past clients while keeping tabs on all of our potential new ones. It would take us hours to send out e-mails, and to cap it all off, we would accidentally be sending the wrong e-mails to the wrong people.

We would bring on new team members and they would quit because they didn't have a good way of keeping up with the work they were doing. We would bring on new customers who would cancel because we looked unprofessional.

We were working our tails off, staying awake long hours, moving incredibly fast—and yet we were losing tens of thousands of dollars every year, all because we didn't have a good system!

And that's when I finally realized that no matter how fast you work, no matter how smart you are, no matter how much passion you have . . .

A company can never outgrow the strength of its systems.

That's when we started looking for something new, and that's when we found Infusionsoft. For us, Infusionsoft was a complete game-changer. It is a system that combines

A company can never outgrow the strength of its systems.

e-mail marketing, customer relationship management (CRM) and e-commerce all into one place.

It is an amazing technology; but it's not the technology that *ultimately* mattered. It was our investment of time and money and energy into figuring out and mapping our own systems. It was reaching a point where we had become truly dedicated to improving our own processes. It was realizing that the *hidden cost* of doing things the way we were doing them was so massive that we finally gave ourselves the *permission* to Invest.

That is the point you need to get to in your life or your business. You won't be able to *multiply* your time until through either pain or perspective you give yourself permission to *Invest.*

And so we did. We invested a great deal of time thinking through what our business really looked like on paper and how the work process would flow.

The first thing we used Infusionsoft for was to fix our follow-up failure. We created supplemental nurture campaigns for almost every part of our business:

- New blog and e-mail subscribers
- New potential recruits
- New prospects
- New customers of each of our one hundred products and services
- Customer service follow-up
- New-hire training

That gave us a chance to maximize the work we were already doing. Once that process multiplied our time by taking care of the people and stakeholders we already had, we automated our *internal* communications. We thought through everything that happens when:

- A new team member is added
- A new customer is welcomed
- A product is delivered
- A customer service issue crops up
- A cross-selling opportunity is identified
- Good news needs to be circulated
- A team works together on a project

It virtually guaranteed perfect communication across our different operating units. It made sure the right people internally were copied on e-mails and everyone else was left off—a worthy miracle in and of itself! Plus, it notified us automatically of our best opportunities of when and how to serve customers.

The magic was happening and we were beginning to feel a tremendous *lift* in our business by having all our systems working in harmony. Similar to compounding interest, it was as though we had amassed a whole new team that was working twenty-four hours a day, seven days a week, making sure that nothing was missed.

We were *compounding our time*. As an entire team, we were *multiplying*.

After we got our initial pile of multiple system chaos fixed, we then turned our focus to amplifying the front end of our business and bringing more people through the front door. And it's amazing the confidence you have when you *know* you can deliver a quality experience *every* time.

Using bestselling author Jay Baer's *Youtility* content strategy system, and a series of Infusionsoft web forums and follow-up sequences, we were able to create a way to set up our system to automatically:

- Get more leads
- Convert more leads
- Create more satisfied customers
- Get repeat sales
- Generate referrals automatically

At first, the task of outlining nearly every company process seemed daunting. But now, looking back, we developed clarity around a critical lesson: Anything you create a process for today saves you time tomorrow.

When all was said and done, the first full year we had the system in place we had doubled our revenue and quadrupled our bottom line! The most valuable part for me, though, was that our team and our customers were getting their best results ever—and meanwhile I finally got my life and my time back.

In full disclosure, I do want to let you know that we became so passionate about the system—after all it did for us—that we became a certified reseller of Infusionsoft. For us, and now some of our other clients, the Internet has become our canvas and Infusionsoft is the paintbrush that helps us make the most of it. If you *are* interested in learning more about Infusionsoft, or you'd like to grab a free download that I created on streamlining your systems, go to infusionsoft.roryvaden.com.

But again, I want to reiterate there is *no* technology that will be your savior.

What will get you going is a *decision* on your part that creating automation is worth it.

It's learning to think like a Multiplier.

Giving yourself the permission to increase your results by investing into your systems.

And it's giving yourself the *permission* to increase your results by investing into your systems.

Hidden cost

Think back to the beginning of this chapter. Do you remember the coffeehouse anecdote about spending the five dollars?

The biggest cost, of course, isn't the five dollars of actual cost.

And it's not the five dollars of opportunity cost.

The biggest cost is the forty-five dollars of *hidden cost*.

But here's the part I really want for you to soak in for a moment . . .

The most expensive part of the equation—the forty-five-dollar cost—is the cost that almost nobody ever even sees!

It is seen only as the result of a *Significance* calculation of compounding interest that most people don't make.

Most people never even factor it into the equation because they are only living in a world of Urgency. They are only paying attention to the here and now. They are thieves who, as a result of their own shortsightedness, are inadvertently stealing from their future selves.

Chapter Summary

Automate: The Permission to Invest

KEY POINTS

- In every transaction there are multiple types of cost:
    - *Actual cost* is the amount of money you actually paid for something.
    - *Opportunity cost* is the equivalent amount of what you gave up by buying something else.
    - *Hidden cost* is the amount of potential return you would've received had you invested that money instead of spent it.
    - *Hidden cost* is the greatest of all of these costs and it is the one that the fewest people ever pay attention to.
- Anything that wastes your time is a waste of your money.
- Many people and companies know they need to invest in better systems but cite "not having the money" or "not having the time" as the reason why they can't. Yet, when you apply the Significance calculation and take time into account, you see that it is literally costing them more not to make the investment. They are missing the permission to Invest.
- A company can never outgrow the strength of its systems.

UNEXPECTED FINDINGS

- Automation is to your time what compounding interest is to your money.

- The greatest threat to anyone's success is not a lack of talent, a lack of education, a lack of resources or a lack of opportunity; it is shortsightedness—a lack of vision. The Significance calculation changes everything.

STARTLING STATISTICS

- The average smoker spends fifteen hundred dollars a year on cigarettes, which invested every year for forty years at 8 percent would be worth $421,172.56.

ACTION QUESTIONS

- What things are you doing over and over again that you could invest time and/or money into automating?

6

Delegate

The Permission of Imperfect

n nature, when baby birds are born they struggle to fight and break through their own shell to get free—to be hatched.

The mama bird *knows* when the baby is alive inside the egg, but if the mama bird or any other force happens to break their egg open *for* them, then once the baby bird is out of the egg, it will attempt to fly but it will fall and die.

This is because the baby bird's wings will not have been developed enough during the hatch. As nature has it, it is the process of their own struggle to break out of their shell that strengthens their wings to the point that they can fly.

It is through the struggle that one develops its strength and independence. And to "help" a bird break out of its shell would be ultimately to cause its death.

This truth is a commonly cited metaphor in personal development because the hatch teaches us an important counterintuitive lesson: Most of the time, it is a service to allow people the natural process of making their own mistakes.

To become a Multiplier, you have to understand and embrace a philosophy similar to the moral of the hatch.

> *It is a service to allow people the natural process of making their own mistakes.*

Why?

Because if you can't Eliminate something—meaning it does need to be done;

And you can't Automate it—meaning you don't yet have the capacity to fully systematize it;

Then the next best thing you can do is Delegate it.

To be a Multiplier is to be a master delegator.

Go through just one day with this question at the forefront of your mind: "Does what I'm doing right now require *my unique* skill set; or is it possible that there are other people capable of doing this?"

If you review an entire day through the lens of that question, you will be shocked at how much of your time is being spent doing things that someone else could be doing for you.

And if you were able to put someone in that position today, she or he would be able to do those tasks for you—to free up that time—tomorrow.

But let's be honest, your challenge probably isn't that you don't *know* you need to delegate more. I mean, you don't have to go through an entire day thinking about this to realize how *much* "stuff" you are doing that someone else could be doing.

No, the problem isn't *knowing* what you should be doing. As is usually the challenge with self-discipline, the hard part is *doing* what you know you should be doing.

Of course the entire *Take the Stairs* methodology is dedicated to teaching you *how to get yourself to do the things you know you should be doing*—so I'd recommend reviewing that, or reading it for the first time if you haven't already.

Here, however, I want to look at *why* you don't Delegate even when you know you *should*.

In fact, I'd bet that you can come up with this answer all on your own.

Tell me, why don't you allow other people to help you do things more often?

You guessed it! Like all the other emotional challenges to multiplying your time, it's fear.

Fear of what?

Fear that it won't be good enough.

Fear that they won't get it done on time.

Fear that it won't meet your level of acceptable standards.

Fear that it wouldn't be as good as you could do it.

And so rather than Delegating, you create yet another story that keeps you perpetually stuck in one-dimensional thinking . . .

You tell yourself, "This would just be faster if I did it myself."

Sound familiar?

(Isn't it eerie how well I *know* you? If you haven't figured it out yet, it's because I am just like you!)

Yes, that is exactly what we tell ourselves. "In the time that I'd have to spend teaching you how to do this, I could've already done it."

Here's the kicker . . . you'd be right!

Once.

You'd be right, if you ignored the Significance calculation.

You'd be right, if you were living in a world of Urgent thinking only about here and now.

But if you use three-dimensional thinking . . .

If you factor in Significance . . .

If you think like a Multiplier . . .

And if you do the actual Multiplier Math . . .

You'd see a different picture entirely.

R.O.T.I.

An executive I sat next to on a plane shared with me this story about the 30x rule:

> *A professor in one of my business classes taught me that "when trying to decide whether to delegate something to someone else or to do something yourself, you should use the thirty-to-one rule."*
>
> *That is, if a daily task took a skilled person like yourself five minutes to complete, you should plan to spend at least a hundred and fifty minutes (five minutes multiplied by thirty) instructing a subordinate how to complete the same task.*
>
> *Now, the hundred and fifty minutes shouldn't all be done at one time and could be spread over a few months as you help the subordinate master the task.*
>
> *He then explained the math behind it:*

"If a task were to take you personally five minutes a day for two hundred and fifty days in a working year, then that means you would spend 1,250 minutes per year on that task.

"Rather than doing that, however, if you decided to spend a hundred and fifty minutes training someone to do that five-minute task, and they instead did that task for you, then that would give you an annual savings of eleven hundred minutes per year."

Simple, but brilliant. The process of spreading out the instruction is something that we at Southwestern Consulting refer to as "spaced-repetition training," and it statistically has a much higher success rate, just as he suggests.

The most powerful part of the story, though, is that although he used the word "spend" all throughout the story, I actually think a more appropriate word would be what we referred to in the last chapter, which was *Invest*.

In fact, I've now been regularly using the acronym "R.O.T.I.," which is short for the phrase "return on *time* invested." Because it *is* an investment *and* it has a tangible, calculable *return* on that investment.

Using the example above, if you take the eleven hundred minutes saved, and you divide that by the hundred and fifty minutes *invested* in training, then you would get a 733 percent return on time invested in one year!

That investment is a no-brainer. Not to mention, I can't imagine a scenario where it would actually take you two and a half hours to teach someone how to do a task that takes five minutes.

And yet, most of us live in a two-dimensional world of "How

does this affect me now?" and we carry around a completely unfounded story that "it would be faster if I did it myself." Meanwhile, we're leaving an investment opportunity with a guaranteed minimum of 733 percent R.O.T.I. on the table.

Although, I guess that is the way of the world, isn't it? The rich get richer because they see things that nobody else sees.

Personal development, motivation and productivity sometimes get criticized for being "soft skills," but there is nothing *soft* about this. Calculating R.O.T.I. is as practical as calculating R.O.I.

Frankly, knowing what we know now—that time is worth much *more* than money—R.O.T.I. is *more* important than R.O.I.

Or maybe I should say is more *Significant* than R.O.I.

Following that thought all the way through also confirms for us mathematically that how you spend your time matters much more than how you spend your money.

How you spend your time matters much more than how you spend your money.

Granted, daily or weekly tasks are easier to see R.O.T.I. on than, say, quarterly or annual tasks. But it's not *necessarily* about the literal application of this math as much as it's about understanding the dynamic view that Multipliers have of the world.

So, knowing that there is a calculable return on time invested in many situations, why aren't you Delegating more of your tasks? I can only think of two reasons:

1. Money
2. Perfectionism

M.V.O.T.

If at this point your big objection to Delegating more of your tasks is that you can't "afford" to actually hire someone to do it, let's look at another mathematical concept.

In the previous chapter on Automate, we discussed the power of compounding interest. A related concept that you've probably heard of if you do any kind of saving or investing is the "Time Value of Money."

Time Value of Money is the calculation used to determine what an amount of money you have today will be worth at some point in the future by adding in an estimated amount of interest or inflation for that time period. For example, in our coffeehouse anecdote, the fifty dollars is the *time value* of five dollars invested at 8 percent for thirty years.

But what about the Money Value of Time?

"Money Value of Time" is a phrase I use to demonstrate another theoretical concept—that there is always another *cost* to participating in any activity.

Every person who earns an income has some hourly wage. Regardless of whether you are paid a salary, straight commission, profit, dividends, bonuses or any other type of compensation plan, we all have an hourly wage. Take a person's annual income and divide it by the number of hours they work in a given year, and you will come up with their hourly rate of pay—the money value of their time (M.V.O.T.). (In the examples below, I've based the math on a 48-week work year and 50 work hours per week.)

Therefore the "cost" of participating in any activity varies among people based on their income and how much time they spend on any given activity. And any time that they are spending on non-income-producing activities has a negative impact on their ability to make more money because it's time they are not spending on things that do generate income.

THE MONEY VALUE OF TIME

ANNUAL INCOME	HOURLY RATE OF PAY (50 hrs/wk)
$40,000	$16.67
$75,000	$31.25
$100,000	$41.66
$150,000	$62.50
$250,000	$104.17
$350,000	$145.83
$500,000	$208.33

Assuming their pay is somehow tied to results:

- Waiting in line for that morning coffee . . . has a cost.
- The time you spend folding laundry or mowing the lawn . . . has a cost.
- Being on hold waiting for a customer service agent . . . has a cost.

The M.V.O.T. concept helps you understand even further the concept of "hidden cost" from the last chapter that "anything that wastes your time *is* a waste of your money." Because in addition to the opportunity cost of the dollars, there is also *always* the opportunity cost of the money value of that time: When you are doing one thing, you are not doing another.

Just to help keep everything organized in your head, this is now a fourth potential cost associated with that coffee:

- Five dollars of actual cost
- Five dollars of opportunity cost
- Forty-five dollars of hidden cost
- Varying amount by person of M.V.O.T. cost—that is, if you make a hundred thousand dollars per year, then that is about forty dollars per hour. So if you spent twenty minutes at the coffee shop, that costs you about thirteen dollars (one third of an hour) of M.V.O.T. cost.

That is getting to be one expensive cup of coffee! One can only hope that the taste, the experience and the customer service you receive are worth it.

The goal of calculating and knowing the Money Value of Your Time is not *necessarily* to make you perpetually evaluate every single second of every day. It also seems like a quite cold and inhumane methodology for how to evaluate the time you spend with other people—although I suppose there is a relevant application even there. But understanding the M.V.O.T. is, again, more of an effort to demonstrate how Multipliers think about time compared to the average person.

On any given day, most people waste a tremendous amount of time. Yet, the more successful the person, the more intentional and protective they seem to be about their time. It's not because they are arrogant, evil, uptight or pompous, but because they have realized that time is one of the truly finite and limited resources. This understanding creates an otherwise unexplainable urgency for them to get things done—and not just at work.

This line of thinking isn't to suggest that work should be the most important thing in your life. But it should be a reality check that the people who seem to get the most out of life are highly conscious, deliberately intentional and relentlessly protective of how they spend their time—because they know there is a great cost.

And as it relates to our discussion here about Delegating, the analysis yields another critical insight:

You are always paying someone to complete a task. You are either paying someone else at their rate of pay, or you are paying yourself at yours.

You are always paying *someone* to complete a task. You are either paying someone else at their rate of pay, or you are paying yourself at yours.

When you say you can't *afford* to pay someone to do the thing you are doing, what you may not realize is that you already are. You are paying you!

So, if you could find someone to do the task that you are doing for less money than your M.V.O.T., you *could* (at least theoretically) afford it because that is what you are paying yourself.

The third permission

If Delegating actually creates substantially more time for you over the long haul (according to the return on time invested—R.O.T.I.—concept) and if you could hire someone to do a task for less than the money value of your own time (M.V.O.T.), then it should be clear that the excuse of "not being able to afford it" isn't the real reason why most of us don't Delegate more often. Thus, we finally get down to what the *real* core issue is about why we have a hard time Delegating: Perfectionism.

Perfectionism isn't a logical issue; it's another emotional one. And like the other elements of fear that we've touched on so far, there is no instantaneously magic cure for it.

I do hope the previous section helps you understand what it is costing you to keep all those tasks to yourself, but at the end of the day, it comes down to your giving yourself the permission of Imperfect.

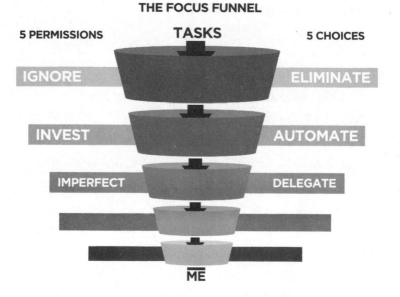

You have to learn to be okay with things just being okay.

You have to embrace the idea that someone else *might* not be able to do it as well as you—at first. But over time, it will get better.

It's fine to always be pushing for progress, but you have to learn to free yourself and anyone around you from the demand for perfection.

You have to give yourself the permission of Imperfect. Remember the story of the hatch: It is a *service* to allow others the natural process of making their own mistakes.

Because what will happen if you don't?

You already know, because it's likely what you have now. You'll have a bunch of perfect useless *stuff* in your life but you are going to be burned out.

You'll be the go-to guy at the office . . . but you'll hate your job.

You'll throw the absolute best parties . . . but you'll resent all your friends.

Your underwear drawer will be folded neatly . . . but you're going to be exhausted.

All of your work will be *perfect* . . . and *you will be miserable!*

I'm the last person who would tell you to do poor-quality work. I would never say to cut corners. But where I failed and what I saw Multipliers doing was empowering the people around them to step up and make a contribution.

They stopped carrying the weight of the world on their shoulders and they invited some teammates to come with them along the way.

They stopped saving the day all the time and empowered other people to also be the hero.

They stopped trying to do it all themselves and instead they created other leaders.

Do you know what happened over time?

The new leaders figured it out. The imperfections got cleaned up. Nobody died. Nothing broke. Nobody went out of business. The house didn't burn down.

In fact, it was just the opposite.

Their results started to *multiply*. And the leaders around them started to *multiply* into other leaders. Things somehow found a way to get done. All the people around chipped in and found a way.

And who got the greatest reward? The Multiplier did! The ones who delegated got some of the pressure taken off of them. And rather than their being one mighty Navy Seal, they built a massive army all around them.

I'm not saying you shouldn't be amazing. I'm not saying you shouldn't produce top-notch work. I'm saying that the best way to do that is to do it through other people and give yourself the permission of knowing it might not be perfect.

Andy Stanley said it best when he said, "Leadership isn't about getting things done *right*. It's about getting things done through *other* people."

Here's some good news from my personal experience. Although I freaked out from time to time and although I've spent way too much time worrying about whether or not little details would ever get taken care of . . . things turn out never to be as bad as they feel or as good as they sound.

They never do.

The crises and the nightmares that come up from time to time always get resolved. The people who make mistakes generally apologize and make up for them. The things that go wrong that we thought would be the end of the world never are.

Things come together and everything is okay.

Things are never as bad as they feel or as good as they sound.

The other good news is that once you learn the power of Delegate, things really start to get fun.

> *Things are never as bad as they feel or as good as they sound.*

LEVERAGING TIME

MULTIPLIER MINDSET CASE STUDY

Troy Peple, Serial Entrepreneur, Accelerent
Washington, DC

It's hard to describe exactly what Troy Peple does. Like the mysterious—but obviously wealthy—"consultant" or "investor" you sat next to on an airplane, or that one friend you have who is definitely successful but you can't quite understand his or her industry or business model, Troy is perfectly happy being filthy rich and totally obscure. He has no desire to be famous or recognized and it doesn't bother him one bit what other people think of him. He only cares about always achieving excellence, doing something *big* and helping multiply the impact of himself and his inner circle.

The only thing more intimidating than his radically fast mental capacity is his appearance—it looks like a 6-foot-6 frame that is stacked with about 250 pounds of solid muscle. At somewhere slightly north of age forty-five, he semi-reluctantly agreed to share his insights with me, and if it hadn't been for us personally connecting and becoming good friends via one of his more recent endeavors, you probably wouldn't be reading this right now. Having succeeded in everything from real estate to appearances in national fitness commercials, he has a robust Rolodex that led him to his newest project that is quickly expanding across the United States: Accelerent.

Unlike networking groups, Accelerent is a high-end private business development platform that helps its members grow their revenue by developing truly meaningful relationships with one another through creating a variety of different structured "environments" for them to meet and engage in. The ultimate goal of this activity is to assist one another in making trusted business introductions to each other's personal contacts. Because only one company from each business category in each city is allowed, their clients can be open in sharing their best relationships.

One of those "environments" is an exclusive local event that brings in a business speaker every month, to which members may invite guests. A big part of Troy's life is now the business of doing something that he has always done, which is surround himself with other successful people.

Like many successful people, Troy started his journey out of adversity.

"My dad was a professor who came from a long line of academics. He didn't have much wealth but he absolutely loved what he did and he was a true scholar. That is, until one day he was unexpectedly let go from the career of his dreams because he hadn't yet received tenure. I watched my dad lose the life that he really wanted because he wasn't in control of his own destiny," Troy recounts.

"So at the age of eight, I resolved that I would be able to retire by age thirty. I got a newspaper route that took me two and a half hours to deliver 275 papers. I finally realized that seventeen of those papers took me forty-five minutes to deliver because they were sparsely scattered along a treacherous and winding road. So I paid another kid to take those off my plate for half of what I was being paid to make the delivery. And *voilà*! Just like that, I stumbled across my first lesson of the money value of time [M.V.O.T.] and the power of delegation.

"At age ten, I discovered there was more margin in cutting lawns, so I switched. At first I was getting twenty dollars to cut pretty big lawns, but then one week we were going to go on vacation and I asked one of my buddies if he'd help me out. He asked me how much I would pay him and I opened my mouth to say 'twenty dollars' but then something made me catch my breath, I paused and said, 'Five dollars.' He said, 'Absolutely!' So he cut three lawns for me for fifteen dollars and I made sixty dollars. After that, I hired as many kids as I could to cut lawns for five dollars, and instead of spending forty hours a week cutting lawns, I spent four hours a week *selling* the cutting of lawns. From that point on, my life was different because I was blessed and lucky to have figured out that certain activities gave me more results in less time; I had discovered how to multiply my time, I had discovered *leverage*.

"I then used some savings and a loan and bought my first rental house at thirteen years old, and by age twenty, I had bought over a million dollars in real estate."

Troy goes on to describe a popular strategy shared by some Multipliers that's sometimes referred to as The Float. "I learned that just like you can leverage your time, you can also leverage 'other people's money' by borrowing at a low interest rate and investing that money into something that will (you hope) give you a higher rate of return and profit from the difference."

As Troy continues talking about "financial leverage" in business, it becomes apparent to me that he and I have opposing philosophies about commercial debt. His financial risk tolerance is obviously higher than mine and what I teach, since he admitted he has "made three fortunes and lost two of them." We disagree on that point, although I don't say it to him directly in the interview—did I mention he looks about 6-foot-6 and 250 pounds? Needless to say, he has ultimately done quite well for himself and we couldn't be more aligned on the concept of leveraging our *time* by developing the skill to delegate, a skill Troy has mastered—even to a fault.

He honestly admits, "Rory, the moment I started reading your book, I immediately knew that it was about me and that I've been a Multiplier my entire life. In fact, I'm such a good Multiplier and delegator that it's gotten to a point where I can actually get into trouble when I'm left with something I can't delegate. If you get really good at getting rid of everything, then if you're not careful you can become really bad at getting things done yourself. One of the guys on my team, Michael, captured it best when he said, 'If Troy is actually *doing* something, then something has gone terribly wrong!'

"And I've realized that he is absolutely right because as the leader, my job isn't to *do*; my job is to make sure that it gets done. My strength is establishing vision, and my contribution is to think and take risk to create more value for everyone. A limiting belief for most people is to think 'no one can do it as well as I can,' and while I have found that to be true, it is only true for a very short while. Once you get past that, you realize that you actually do a lesser quality job than another person could do who specializes in that task. I've learned that if you give people the authority to manage an area, even if they aren't *that* good at first, eventually they will *get* good. And 80 percent done by everybody else is always better than 100 percent done by me. Similarly, I know that with my skill set, I am infinitely better off owning 10 percent of ten businesses that other people run, than owning 100 percent of things that I have to run."

In hindsight, I realize that Troy is one of the most fascinating thinkers I have ever met. And as I look over the

> *As the leader, my job isn't to do; my job is to make sure that it gets done.*

landscape of all he has accomplished in his career, I'm amazed at the number of millionaires he has created all around him through such a diverse set of initiatives. Indeed, I am inspired by the number of instances in which his delegation abilities empowered people to reach levels they never thought possible. His delegation allowed them to become the brilliant, capable individuals they were born to be. Finally it dawns on me that perhaps Troy Peple's full-time job isn't so mysterious after all . . . he is, simply, a Multiplier.

The business of you

Delegating seems to be one of the most obvious of the Multiplier strategies, since you create more time for yourself tomorrow by having someone else do the task. But because the emotional struggle with perfection is so strong for so many of us, it is sometimes the last strategy that people really master.

Another paradigm shift I experienced from spending time around Multipliers was that I was amazed at how they viewed their own individual lives in a nearly identical fashion to how they viewed their businesses.

In particular, they applied the same principles of multiplying their time in their businesses to multiplying their time in various aspects of their own personal lives.

Think for a moment about all the various professions that it takes or could take to manage the aspects of your personal affairs:

- **Office assistant:** Having an office assistant when you've never had one before will absolutely change your life. You never realize how much time you spend mailing, copying, printing, searching and so on. If your business model and structure allows for it, this is one of the first investments you should make.

- **Business coach:** Multipliers almost always have coaches. Because they have figured out that if they can learn from someone else's mistakes, pay someone else to take the time to filter the most valuable personal development content, have someone hold them accountable and push them to the next level, and use someone else's advice to keep them from doing something foolish, then that is a great first investment. If you're open to investing in your own business coach and you'd like to have a free call to learn about it, visit coaching.roryvaden.com.

- **Accountant:** You must have a good accountant. As you incorporate the principles in this book, you are going to *multiply* your results, which also means you are going to start *multiplying* your wealth. You are going to need a good accountant in your "personal organization" to answer questions and advise you. And when it comes to doing your taxes just think "how many hours will it take me times my hourly M.V.O.T." and if that is more than what it would cost to have an accountant do it, then let them do it.

- **Bookkeeper:** This is one of the best investments my wife, Amanda, and I made recently. And similar to an assistant, it will rock your world the first time you find a good one. Different from an accountant, this is someone who you can hand a stack of receipts and they scan them, create your expense reports, compile spending reports and do the initial legwork of your tax preparation every year.

- **Financial planner:** Another must-have. Even if you are just starting your journey of multiplying your wealth, it still is good to connect with a good advisor. It should be someone whose philosophy aligns with your long-term plan, who doesn't intimidate you when you ask questions and whom you really trust.
- **Lawyer:** Got to have one. And it helps to have one that you know but don't need so that when you actually do need one, she or he is there.
- **Insurance agent:** There are hundreds of different types of insurance. There are only a few that you really need. Check out Dave Ramsey's book *The Total Money Makeover* for a more detailed education.
- **Real estate agent:** This is someone you want in your "personal organization." Once you are debt-free, buying "paid-for" real estate is going to become an important part of your portfolio. Like most of the people on this list, you can think of her or him as an "on-call" independent contractor with whom you have a relationship but you don't pay until you really need them.
- **Graphic designer:** I've been surprised how often I am in need of something professionally created that looks great. It's useful to have an ongoing relationship with someone you can trust. For simple projects, there is a great website called "99designs" that is worth checking out.

- **Travel coordinator:** Depending on how much you travel, this can turn into a full-time job. It takes an incredible amount of time to review flight options, find hotels and secure rental cars. This is something you *have* to Delegate. If you have one primary office assistant, then he or she can do many of these things for you in the beginning; but give yourself the permission to invest more and ramp up your "personal organization" as needed.

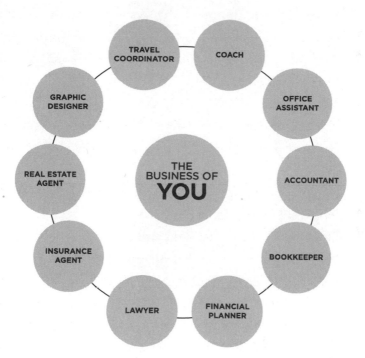

One key is to remember the 30x rule. Sometimes you will have to invest time into training these people and it will be frustrating if they quit or leave or you have to change, but it's worth it. You're not just thinking about the time today. As a Multiplier, you think in terms of Significance and you are thinking about all the time this will affect in the future.

I realize that not every person is in a position in his or her life where they have someone to delegate *to*, but these principles can still apply to you. Because, no different from your professional life, you also need to assemble a team for your personal life.

Here are some other roles that you might consider Delegating:

- **House cleaner:** The moment you can afford it, this is a total no-brainer. If you want to immediately improve your marriage, invest in a house cleaner. It makes you feel good, it keeps things organized and, based on the M.V.O.T. calculation, it makes *so* much sense.

- **Nanny:** Another critical investment. I'm not promoting that you outsource raising your kids, but the number of insignificant tasks that have to do with raising kids is mind-boggling. Maximize your time with them and make it count by getting some help for the trivial tasks.

- **Gardener:** What is the significance of having short, green grass? Unless it is a hobby that you enjoy and derive peace from, invest in someone to help you do this. Spend that time on something that *multiplies*. The kid down the street will do it for ten bucks.

- **Grocery (or personal) shopper:** While this might seem like an extravagant item, these days it's quite common to have someone help you with your shopping. This can be in the form of a fashion stylist (which some department stores offer as a free service because theirs are paid on commission) to someone to run to the store and pick up your weekly grocery staples. There are also online services that can handle these tasks for you.

- **Mechanic:** Lord knows I'm not getting underneath any cars—it would mess up my hair. Seriously, the amount of time I'd have to spend to learn how to change a taillight would probably make the M.V.O.T. astronomical. If it isn't your hobby, leave it to the professionals.
- **Personal assistant:** Dry cleaning. Post office. Gift wrapping. Grocery store. Enough said. Create a job for someone around you! That is what Multipliers do . . .
- **Handyman:** Does it really save you that much money to spend three hours installing the ceiling fan yourself? One word . . . M.V.O.T.
- **Driver:** If you spend a lot of time in the car—the average travel time to work in the United States is 25.4 minutes[*] per trip and sitting in traffic accounts for 38 hours per year[†]—the first thing you can do to *multiply* your time is listen to audio books or podcasts (I have a weekly show!). The next level, though, is to have a driver so that you can completely focus on making the most of your time. There is a reason CEOs, presidents and other high performers make this investment: That time is worth a lot.

---

[*] "Average Commute Times," WNYC, project.wnyc.org/commute-times-us/embed.html#5.00/42.000/-89.500.

[†] Adam Werbach, "The American Commuter Spends 38 Hours a Year Stuck in Traffic," *Atlantic*, February 6, 2013, theatlantic.com/business/archive/2013/02/the-american-commuter-spends-38-hours-a-year-stuck-in-traffic/272905.

- **Chef:** Cooking is another one of those things that gives a lot of people enjoyment and peace. If that is the case, then of course *don't* Delegate it. But if not, consider getting a personal chef to come over a couple times a week. There has also been a rise in "fresh home food delivery" services. Maybe this could just be a supplemental way to save time or something you just do every once in a while.

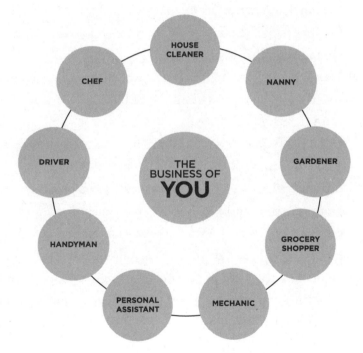

After reviewing a list like the one above, it becomes apparent that anyone who runs a household runs a business! If you are a stay-at-home mom or dad, you are running a business—and it's big business. Look at all of the people "around the table" it takes to make everything work. So take pride in your business.

If you are not able to pay money to someone to get help with different things happening in your life, you

Anyone who runs a household runs a business!

should still try to be creative about ways to apply this principle. Just because you don't have a lot of money doesn't mean you can't find help. For example, and I may be overstepping my bounds here, but if you are a parent and you have kids, put them to work!

I think it was Bill Cosby who said, "The first time my kid looked at me and said he didn't want to do chores, I looked back at him and said, 'What do you think I brought you into this world for, son?!'"

Kids are already the most expensive part of your payroll, right? You might as well put them to work, and although they may not like it, you'll be preparing them to be more successful in life later on. Just don't be afraid to allow them to make their own mistakes with some of your projects.

You don't have to have a lot of extra cash to start building a team of people around you. My first office assistant was a virtual one that worked for six dollars an hour. In fact, you don't have to have any money to start building a team. If you can create a vision for a project, then you can inspire people to want to help contribute to the success of that project. So develop the skill of creating an inspiring vision and then ask people to join up with you to help achieve it. You can even offer to pay them later based on the success of the project.

Whether it's in your professional life or your personal life, the size of your success is usually determined by the strength of your team. So fill in your gaps and supplement your weaknesses by bringing on other people. Invest the time (and money) to train them properly. Give yourself and them the permission of Imperfect and start making progress by doing more together as a team.

Because from here on out, it's all up to you . . .

Chapter Summary

Delegate: The Permission of Imperfect

KEY POINTS

- It is a service to allow people the natural process of making their own mistakes.
- The reason we don't Delegate is because of a false belief that "someone else won't be able to do it as well as I can" or that "it is faster to do it myself."
- R.O.T.I. stands for "return on time invested," and it works the same as an R.O.I. calculation of money except it is for your time.
- M.V.O.T. stands for Money Value of Time and articulates that all of us have an hourly wage and that we are always either paying someone else at their rate of pay to complete a task, or we are paying ourselves at ours.

UNEXPECTED FINDINGS

- Andy Stanley teaches us that "Leadership isn't about getting things done right. It's about getting things done through other people."
- Anyone who runs a household runs a business.
- The 30x rule says that we should invest 30 times the amount of time it takes to complete a task in training someone to do the task and it will still be worth it.
- Most of us drastically underestimate the number of skills it takes to just keep up with our daily lives and the incredible

opportunity of creating jobs for others and peace for ourselves by learning to outsource.

STARTLING STATISTICS

- Someone who makes a hundred thousand dollars a year has
  an M.V.O.T. of $41.66, so being on hold for twenty minutes
  when they could be working costs them about thirteen
  dollars.

ACTION QUESTIONS

- What tasks are you hanging on to that you need to let go
  control of?

7

Procrastinate

The Permission of Incomplete

f you went to a lake and found an experienced fisherman at dusk, what would you see lying right next to his feet strung together near the edge of the water?

Well, you'd see a six-pack of beer!

But what would you see next to that?

Yes, you'd probably see a full line of all the fish he had caught so far.

What if you went to the lake at eleven a.m. instead? How many fish do you think he'd have on his line?

You probably wouldn't see many fish—if any at all. In fact, you probably wouldn't even see any fishermen there. Why not?

Because there are no fishermen fishing at eleven a.m.—because fish aren't biting at eleven a.m.!

The fish are biting at dawn and at dusk.

You could go fishing at eleven a.m. and cast as many lines into the water as you want—that is, work as hard as you can and as fast as you can—but you simply won't get the same results as you would with that same amount of energy applied in the morning or in the evening.

It seems so obvious when analyzing this story, yet many of us completely ignore the lesson of fishermen in our daily lives.

That is, any level of skill is amplified by appropriate timing.

Notice that to be a great fisherman, the proper question is not so much "Am I fishing the right amount of time?" but "Am I fishing at the *right* time?"

Any level of skill is amplified by appropriate timing.

Here is another question for you: Do you think the fisherman who is fishing at dusk stops to clean each one of the fish right after he catches them?

Of course not.

Why doesn't the fisherman clean the fish?

Because that would waste the precious limited time he has to catch all the fish when they are biting.

Now, do you think the fisherman will eventually clean all the fish that he catches?

Obviously, he will.

But here is the point that we often miss: It is possible to do the right thing at the wrong time.

- You don't want to sell your house when the real estate market is awful.
- You don't want to start a business when you just had a baby.
- You don't want to launch a line of new bathing suits at Christmastime.

- And you don't want to plan a family vacation in March if you're a tax accountant!

Timing matters.

A Multiplier knows that it's not just about *what* to do, or *how much* to do.

It's also about *when*.

As we have been moving through the Focus Funnel, each stage has presented us with a critical question to answer.

In the Eliminate stage, it was, "Is this task something I can live without?"

In the Automate stage, it was, "Can this task be systematized?"

In the Delegate stage, it was, "Can this task be performed by someone else?"

If the answer to those three questions is no, then guess what?

That means it's a task that is all yours. (Finally, you get to do something!)

Since the task belongs to you, the last thing to figure out is whether to complete the task now or later.

The corresponding critical question to ask, then, is a brilliant question that we typically *only* ask someone when we are completely overwhelmed and frustrated, but I want you to ask it intentionally, and that question is . . .

"Can this wait until later?"

And, if the answer to that question is yes, then . . .

Get ready for it . . .

I want you to . . .

I'm inviting you to . . .

I am challenging you to . . .

Actually . . .

Procrastinate on purpose!

Yes, I am asking you to wait!

I'm suggesting that you *not* take action. I'm encouraging you to *not* do it.

Patience and procrastination

You might say, "Now wait just a minute, Rory! In *Take the Stairs* you said, 'Action is ultimately the inevitable prerequisite for our success,' and now you're telling me to *not* take action?

"Not to mention that in chapter three of this book you said I should channel my emotion into the excellence of doing something rather than the mediocrity of deciding whether or not to do it, and now you are encouraging me to *not* do some things?"

I know, and that is all accurate exactly how I said it in the context of one thing: *timing*.

But there is a subtle yet very significant distinction to make. We often confuse . . .

Waiting to do something because we know it is something that we *should* do but we don't really *want* to do it . . .

with . . .

. . . waiting because we decide that *now* is not the *right* time.

The first is unconsciously delaying because we aren't looking forward to it.

The second is intentionally delaying because we determine the timing is wrong.

The first is procrastination.

But the second is *patience*.

There is a big difference between inaction that results from indulgence, and inaction that results from intention; one is procrastination and the other is patience.

And there is a synonym for *Procrastinate on Purpose* and that is . . . *patience*.

Patience is giving yourself time to breathe.

Patience is giving yourself margin in your life and not trying to do everything.

Patience is slowing things down.

Patience is taking a moment to gather perspective.

Patience is letting it sit while you focus on something bigger.

But when . . .

You know you should be making that sales call and you're afraid. That's procrastination.

You know you should be going to the gym and you're not. That's procrastination.

You know you need to have that difficult conversation and you haven't. That's procrastination.

You know you should be doing it now and you're not doing it—that's procrastination!

Thus, this is the critical intersection point between *Take the Stairs* and *Procrastinate on Purpose* because they both have the same message:

Do the things you know you should be doing!

Take the Stairs was all about how to do that.

This book is about what to do with everything else so you can get down to *that*.

What you may not have realized up until now—I didn't—is that the two books are interconnected. But here's the thing, *Procrastinate on Purpose* is not the *sequel* to *Take the Stairs*; it's the *prequel*.

Really, it's the other side of the coin.

Procrastinate on Purpose is about the patience to *wait*. *Take the Stairs* is about the discipline to *act*.

And in order to *multiply your time*, you don't need just one; you need both!

Success in your life is not black and white. It's not a straightforward system with a correct set of answers. It's a constantly conflicting conundrum of counteracting forces.

It's fast and slow.

It's big and small.

It's logic and emotion.

It's patience and it's action.

And your ultimate compass is your own *spirit*. It's about listening and trusting what it says to you and how it guides you and *doing the things you know you should be doing*.

Patience is a great discipline indeed.

Last minute

Your next question might be, "Okay, Rory, so you want me to wait if I can, but you don't want me to wait until the last minute, right?"

Actually, waiting until the last possible minute is *exactly* what I want you to do!

Now, I know chances are that reading that last line might be a bit of a shock to your system. Initially, "waiting until the last minute" might not *seem* like something that is a good idea or something that you are comfortable with.

But don't freak out just yet.

You don't associate the "last minute" with the actual "last minute."

You most likely connect "waiting until the last minute" with meaning late nights, extra shipping costs, added stress, unplanned adjustments and the like.

That kind of "last minute" isn't *really* the "last minute." That is *after* the last minute.

The "last minute" that Multipliers use is not the last possible minute to get something done. Just as a "yes" to the question "Can this wait until later?" implies, *now* is not the final opportunity to start and still complete things successfully and peacefully and at the *right time*.

If waiting until later *would* actually cause you to sacrifice the integrity of whatever the task is at hand, then the answer to "Can this wait until later?" wouldn't be yes, it would be no.

So the "last minute" here is really "the last minute that you can afford to wait until later and still get exactly what you wanted done without causing any damage."

And indeed, the precise moment that waiting until later would cause you to sacrifice something would be the moment when the answer to the question "Can this wait until later?" becomes "No, it cannot wait until later." And *when* that happens, the task will pass through that checkpoint question and drop down to the final stage of the Focus Funnel.

At *that* moment it will then become a priority Concentrate—which we'll get to later.

So, your next question might be, "Okay, Rory, even so, why would you want to wait until the last minute? Why not finish things the first possible moment the opportunity arises?"

And that is a great question. In fact, I had the same exact question when I first realized this very counterintuitive methodology of Multipliers.

Why in the world would you want to *wait*?

The answer we finally inferred from them is because . . .

Things change.

Plans change.

Dates change.

Prices change.

Legislation changes.

Technology changes.

Strategy changes.

Weather changes.

In our multifaceted, incredibly dynamic, always nimble and insanely fast culture today, things are *always* changing!

And if you take action too *early*, you might be adversely affected later by *unexpected change* when it could have been avoided.

Think back to the Eliminate section. You'll recall we said that whenever possible, resisting making unnecessary change today saves you drastic amounts of time tomorrow.

Well, here, in this situation, it's not so much that *our* plans

might change—although they might—but some *external* factor
might create unexpected change:

- A customer ordered a thousand units of *X* products and you
  boxed it up two weeks early, and then your salesperson calls
  to say they upped the order: You suddenly have extra rework
  cost.
- You ordered twenty thousand extra units of *Y* products so
  that you have "plenty on hand," but then two months later
  your competitor launches a product that renders yours obso-
  lete: You suddenly have a huge carrying cost.
- You were eager to get that new flyer printed and you got a
  great deal on printing in bulk, but then two weeks later you
  decided you needed to reposition your whole marketing
  message: You suddenly have a massive sunk cost.
- You finally had some money set aside to Angel-invest and,
  of your three choices, you took the first one that really
  opened the door to you . . . and the other majority investors
  replaced the CEO with a new guy who tanked the company. Meanwhile, the other two opportunities you didn't
  wait for hit it big: You suddenly have an unfortunately large
  hidden cost.

These are just a few examples that happen every day. They are
all examples of "*unexpected change cost*." And with everything moving as fast as it is moving right now, unexpected change is a very
real cost that is eating up and destroying companies.

But the cost of unexpected change doesn't just affect businesses.
It affects our personal lives:

- You emptied your checking account into a brand-new car that you drove off the lot and three days later got approached to buy a short-sale house at a 75 percent discount before it went to auction and now you don't have the money: You suddenly have a painful opportunity cost.
- You wanted so badly to have a project ready that you forced yourself to create it too soon. Your ideas and your platform didn't have time to develop and materialize, and you didn't have the distribution setup in place: You have rework cost.
- You were in love with the idea of being in love and you rushed and got married only to find out later that you changed, and the other person changed: You have every type of cost imaginable!

I was completely blind and oblivious to this whole dynamic of unexpected change cost too until one of our consulting clients— and classic entrepreneurial Multiplier from the previous chapter— Troy Peple said casually in a meeting: "Whenever possible, I never take an action that can't be untaken until either I *have* to or until there is an overwhelmingly compelling reason that I *should*."

So, you definitely don't want to be late.

But you also don't want to be too early.

A Multiplier works to be precisely on time.

A Multiplier works to be precisely on time.

Things have changed . . .

It used to be:

Early is "on time"

On time is "late"
and Late is "You're fired!"

But now:
Late is still "You're fired!"
but
Early is risky
and
Last minute is right on time.

Early makes you vulnerable because it's an underutilization of your most limited asset: time.

You want another example of something that wealthy people *never* do that I've done (wrong) almost my entire life?

Wealthy people *never* pay their bills or their taxes early.

Why?

Because they live in a world of Significance calculations. And they know that any time they pay early, then someone else can be investing that money over the time spread between when they paid and when their payment is actually due. Which means that someone else is getting the hidden benefit of the time value of *their money*.

Again, they don't want to pay their bills late because they don't want the costs of interest or additional fees, just like the rest of us, but they will never pay early, either. Their goal is to wait till the "last minute"—which is precisely on time.

Doing something early is not the same as creating more time. It is just taking time from tomorrow and moving it into today and adding the risk of unexpected change cost.

When I say that *multiplying* your time is "spending time on things today that will create more time tomorrow" I am suggesting that something you are doing today is *altering* how it will be done tomorrow or eliminating it from being done tomorrow; not that you simply move it to be "earlier" in time. Time is our most powerful and most limited asset, and we want to take full advantage of it.

Visually it might look something like this:

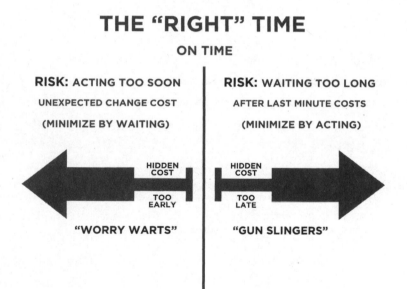

Gun Slingers and Worry Warts

Some of the companies we consult with and some of the people we coach at Southwestern Consulting are what we call "Gun

Slingers." They have no fear about waiting till the last minute. Truth be told, they are often just fine operating in a mode of "*after the last minute*" and waiting until the night before it's due. It's pretty much their MO (modus operandi) and has been most of their lives.

Gun Slingers never run the risk of acting too early, but they may act too late. Gun Slingers need to be cautious about coming across as sloppy and unplanned. And they may occasionally make a foolish—usually expensive—decision because they waited too long and then didn't have the time to evaluate it completely. Gun Slingers sometimes come in late and rowdy and start firing off bullets everywhere; they can be crazy-makers.

Gun Slingers often miss out on the benefit of compounding interest because they live in a sometimes incorrectly calculated frivolous mindset of "I can just wait until later and it'll be fine."

But on the other hand, Gun Slingers usually do not run the risk of exposing themselves to "unexpected change cost" by acting too early. If we're all lucky, they will at best be on time; but we can pretty much count on the idea that they're never early.

Gun Slingers need no help with this *Procrastinate on Purpose* section. They've got this part down! But they should be sensitive to how they come across to those around them.

We have other clients who are "Worry Warts." They never want to wait till the last minute. They *always* want to complete a task as soon as possible. Action is great, but the danger is that they are at risk of acting too hastily and making themselves and their organizations vulnerable to unexpected change cost.

They might get everyone locked into something too early, which then creates a bunch of rework for everyone later on. Or they miss out on a "last-minute" savings opportunity from a vendor because they wanted to "get it done so they can move on to the next thing" rather than patiently negotiating.

Another challenge for Worry Warts is that they take pride in getting everything done ahead of schedule. What often ends up happening, though, is that they are driving projects much faster than the people around them are able to keep up with. So *they* get it done, and in *their* mind they *think* it's all over. But then later everyone else finally catches up and they would have liked to have had input or shared their ideas as to how to make the project better and since they didn't get a chance to do that beforehand now they want to change it.

This dynamic creates *incredible stress* for Worry Warts because now *they* have to do *their* work over again and in their mind it's the result of everyone else "always waiting till the last minute."

Sometimes it *is* true that the people around them *are* waiting until *after* the last minute—and when that happens the Worry Warts' frustration is warranted.

But other times it is the Worry Warts' fear of waiting till the last minute that is the very thing subjecting them to the pain of unexpected change cost. Even though they don't see it this way, they have no one else to blame but themselves. They are in need of patience and they need the permission of the Incomplete.

Contrary to how our workplace interactions sometimes transpire, though, neither Gun Slingers nor Worry Warts are jerks that are out to make life as hard as possible for the other. Rather, they are simply people with varying levels or different types of risk tolerance; and you need *both* of them on your team to be successful.

They are naturally counteracting forces that are critical in making sure you don't act too soon and you don't wait too long. It is their perpetual conflict that creates the healthy order of helping you determine when the "right on time" actually is.

The fourth permission

Those of us Worry Warts are the ones who have the challenge with *Procrastinate on Purpose.* The whole idea of "waiting till the last minute" almost seems to scrape against the fabric of our very soul. It is not in our *nature* to wait.

As a result, many Worry Warts are some of the most successful people you've ever met. These are people who are *doers.* They *get stuff done.* In times of chaos, people look to them to bring order. And in their mind a core reason for their own success may very well be that they are checklisters who always take action without delay.

In fact, if one had to choose between a default of not taking action and one of taking action, then my recommendation would definitely be to have a predisposition toward the latter. It is becoming pervasively common, however, for Worry Warts to be "carrying the weight of the world." They feel exorbitant pressure to always act and act *now.* It's almost as if they have a nonstop nagging voice inside their own head reminding themselves of everything they have to do and all the deadlines coming up.

They may have even come to rely on that voice for a sense of drive, since it is how they have propelled themselves to get where they are now. But minus the ability to let go of it, that same voice will be the thing that ultimately limits getting to the next level as a Multiplier.

Worse than that, it is that voice, that internal sense of impending doom, that will steal the joy in their life.

It will create a heavier and heavier weight of stress. It may push them to "success," but then it will push them more, and more, and more. It will push them faster and faster and faster. And they will get more and more done but feel less and less in control.

Always a new deadline.

Always a new project.

Always something to do trying desperately to stay ahead of schedule.

Until one day it pushes them so hard that they finally . . .

Burn out.

Or . . .

Something else will happen.

They will realize that the thing driving them is not a *real* deadline; it's an imaginary one.

They will see that staying "ahead of schedule" is not what their true goal is; it's a façade.

They will understand that the very thing they've relied on is what they have to let go of.

And if they are incredibly lucky, they will stop for a moment . . .

And finally come to grips with where the pressure they feel is *really* coming from . . .

Their own fear of not being good enough.

And in that moment it will make sense to them, perhaps for the first time ever, that no amount of tasks being completed, no amount of trophies being won and no amount of dollars being collected will ever release them from that *story* that has been holding them hostage for all these years.

Rather, all they have to do is simply make a decision to give themselves the permission of the Incomplete.

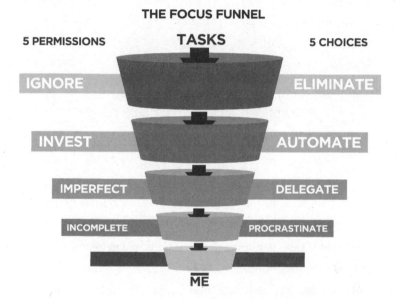

THE FOCUS FUNNEL

5 PERMISSIONS · TASKS · 5 CHOICES

IGNORE — ELIMINATE

INVEST — AUTOMATE

IMPERFECT — DELEGATE

INCOMPLETE — PROCRASTINATE

ME

The permission of the Incomplete means that they will realize that their work is never done. That *everything* is always a work in progress. This permission lets you know that even when things seem "finished," they are not. And that there is no finish line, but there also is *no* deadline.

> *There is no finish line, but there also is no deadline.*

They will learn to be okay with things being *just okay*. They will embrace the idea that things really can be "good enough." They will finally give up their struggle to control . . . and peace will come rushing in.

Once and for all, they will finally be free of that pressure that Charles Hummel called "The Tyranny of the Urgent."

And so they will move on graciously and buoyantly, at a comfortable pace, *waiting* for the "right time" rather than *forcing* it.

URGENCY OR EMERGENCY?

MULTIPLIER MINDSET CASE STUDY

Michael Book, Financial Services, MassMutual

New York, New York

No matter who you are, when you have a question about your money or your investments, you want an answer and you want it fast. Which means that if you are Michael Book and you are the general agent of a team of a hundred and thirty producers that has well over $2 billion in assets under management, a huge fee-based planning practice, and that sold $4 billion of new life insurance last year . . . you have a lot of high-net-worth people who want your time *right this second*.

The Book Agency is—and has been for several years— the number one agency in the nation for the well-respected MassMutual Financial Group. I've been to their office multiple times, and I can tell you personally that on any given day, Michael gets several hundred e-mails, and will consistently get interrupted by five to ten people pushing aggressively for unscheduled time with him in between an already completely slated calendar. Charismatic, sharp and confident, Michael moves and speaks with certainty about how he has become an ultra-performer and a Multiplier.

"My most important role is being available to our relationship managers [his term for producer or salesperson] and so I count on that as a key part of my day. My job is not doing paperwork; my job is being with people. I need to talk to our relationship managers to make sure they have the tools they need to do their job. With a hundred and thirty people coming to me for advice virtually non-stop, however, I do have a gatekeeper and some very deliberate philosophies," he begins.

"What you have to realize is that today the vast majority of the pressures you feel in your life are not from your emergencies; they are from other people putting their urgency on you—and you can't let that happen. I don't let other people's urgency become mine unless I decide that it really is an emergency and I am their only solution. It's almost like I'm in a constant calculation of determining 'what *really* does have to happen now that is going to have the greatest *long-term* impact?' In fact, it's a lot like triage."

Wanting more, I prod a bit harder to try and get insider access into this subconscious process that he has obviously mastered. I press, "But *how* do you make that calculation? How do you know who and what to take on now, and who and what to let go?"

"The biggest thing I try to quickly figure out—whether it be via written form, them communicating through my gatekeeper, or when they burst through my door—is whether or not this is a matter of 'Urgency' or 'Emergency.'" All of this stumbles out as if he is articulating this brilliant strategy for the first time ever—even to himself.

"And the difference between the two?" I ask.

"'Urgency' is someone just wanting the immediate gratification of an instant answer or completing something for the sake of completing it. 'Emergency' is something truly significant that must be dealt with right now because there is a substantially negative impact of dealing with it later. When someone needs me to sign off on something so they can submit a file, that is Urgency—regardless of why they try to sell me it has to happen this minute. I'll put that off until later all day long. On the other hand, when a valuable client who could refer a lot of business or is high profile is sitting in our lobby to meet with one of our new agents and there are no other experienced people to help partner on that meeting—that is an Emergency and I'll immediately engage.

"The simple litmus test, which I am constantly challenging people with, is 'Can this wait until later?' When I *force* people to answer that question for themselves, they realize on their own that the answer is usually, 'Yes, it can wait until later.' If it can wait until later, then it should and we will create a game plan for how and when to deal with it, but we don't do it right then.

"Urgency is much more common than Emergency. Urgency is typically the result of someone losing perspective (in our case it's usually because a client has put pressure on my relationship manager) and becoming *emotional* about *wanting* an answer or solution now—when they really don't *need* it right this second. Emergency is when something that will have a long-term or substantial impact is *truly* affected by a short-term window of opportunity. Trying to help people delineate between the two is an important part of my job, but allowing them to put their Urgency on me when it is not an Emergency definitely isn't," he clarifies.

I then ask, "Does the same methodology apply to which people you take meetings with now and which ones you delay until later?"

"Many people have some guilt about accepting this, but the answer is 'Of course!' Now, generally speaking, if any one of my guys thinks it's an Emergency for them, then that makes it Urgent enough for me to consider how I can help them. I may bail them out once with a clear expectation that they shouldn't wait until after the last minute next time so that we aren't in this predicament again. But there is no doubt that you have to prioritize your time with people.

"If I'm sitting with one of my top guys—or someone who is really brand-new with the potential to become a top producer—and someone else comes in asking me for something, I'm likely not going to allow the interruption. Similarly, if I'm sitting with someone else and one of my big and experienced producers comes in and says, 'I have an emergency that needs to be dealt with right now,' I'm going to ask if it can wait until later (if they are experienced, hopefully they have already asked that question). If it can't wait until later, then I'm going to allow the interruption. It's important for my top people to get the feeling that I am there to help them as problem solver. It's not a matter of me playing favorites; it's a responsibility I have to use my time in a way that is best for the success of the entire team.

"It doesn't just apply to producers, either. If it's a staff person who has shown signs of making a significant long-term difference to our organization, then I'm going to invest my time with them. For example, when I know that if I spend time with that person, they will quickly learn it and be able to make those decisions on their own moving forward without having to come to me, I'm going to protect that time. One way of saying it, I suppose, is that I'm very passionate about treating everyone fairly—but not necessarily equally.

> *I'm very passionate about treating everyone fairly—but not necessarily equally.*

"My ultimate responsibility is to always be looking down the road to what is going to create the best success for the entire organization. I can write checks to make problems go away, but I can't write checks to get me more time. Therefore I need to be constantly calculating and certifying that—at any given moment—I am spending my time on things that are going to grow the organization for everyone. I need to be investing my time now into things that are going to give our team the greatest return in the future . . . everything else is simply going to have to wait."

Popping and batching

It is a bit of an irony that 91 percent of people claim to have a general belief that things will work out for the best and yet we rush around frantically so often to try and satisfy our fear that things will fall apart if we don't.* The Multiplier mindset teaches us that it is *okay* to wait.

We can slow down a little bit.

Nothing is ever as bad as it feels or as good as it sounds. The world won't come to an end. The company won't go out of business.

And it is not only healthy for your soul, but there is also *multiplication* power in creating space, time and margin in your life. It enables your ideas to incubate and for you to get a bit of perspective. It reduces the vulnerability of unexpected change. Sometimes the act of waiting today is the very thing that prevents you from doing something you would have had to redo tomorrow.

---

*Focused 40 Survey conducted by Southwestern Consulting in 2012–2013.

You may or may not have authority in your work life to decide which projects get to wait and which ones don't, but this principle still applies to you. No matter who you are, you have some control, even if it is over the tiniest details relating to one specific project. And we all have control over how we decide to use our time outside of work. So what are some of the things that we can Procrastinate on today to create more time tomorrow?

Let's take a look at some examples:

- **Paying bills and taxes:** We already covered this and it is a surprisingly consistent habit of wealthy people.
- **Placing large orders:** It is a common "best practice" among Multipliers to wait as long as possible before placing huge orders. This is to allow themselves as much time as possible to prevent unexpected change cost.
- **Spending big money:** Another consistent piece of advice you will hear from people who are wise with wealth is to *always* "wait at least one night" before making a big financial purchase. Part of the reason this is wise is because one of the most frequent elements in unexpected change is that our *feelings* change. In general, the bigger the decision, the more time you should give it to marinate and mature.
- **Waiting out uncertainty:** If you're not at least 75 percent sure of what the right decision is—don't make one. Very similar to what was mentioned earlier in the chapter, you need to be mindful of whether or not your delay is intentional in order to minimize unexpected change cost

(patience) or if it's because you *know* what the right decision is and you're just putting it off because you don't want to make it (procrastination).

- **Recognizing false alarms:** A leader is a Multiplier and Multipliers are leaders, so as a leader, you will be the recipient of people's problems. Understand that their problem is *always* going to *seem* urgent to them. With your new vantage point of the Significant perspective, however, you should immediately reduce the times you get *sucked* into their "fires." It likely won't behoove you to tell *them* this, but you should purposely put off engaging in things that will seem like "fires"—because of the emotion in which they are presented to you—when they really aren't. As a Multiplier,

> *As a Multiplier, you are no longer just a Fire Fighter; you are a Seed Planter.*

you are no longer just a Fire Fighter; you are a Seed Planter. Things that get other people in a tizzy shouldn't have the same impact on you because you will have a longer-term (Significance) perspective.

The list above represents just a few of the major things that we see coming up on a regular basis for our coaching and consulting clients that can be "Popped"—a term we use that is short for *Procrastinated on Purpose.* The better you get at this, the more you will find a growing number of activities in your life and your business that can really be "Popped" without causing any damage. They *can* wait.

Just as the diagram suggests, when you "POP" an activity, you shoot it back up to the top of the Focus Funnel.

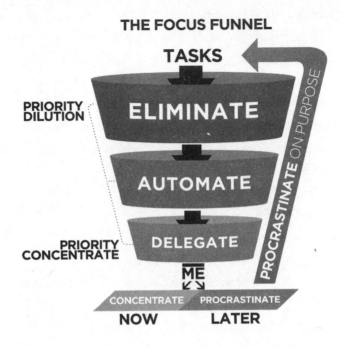

The Popped activity will then enter into a holding pattern, circling back through the Focus Funnel. Every so often you will find the activity cropping up at the top of your To Do pile or to the "top of your mind" for you to evaluate—based upon the checkpoint questions—once again:

- Is it something that you can live without? (Eliminate)
- Is it something that can be systematized? (Automate)
- Can it be done by someone else? (Delegate)
- Can it wait until later? (Procrastinate)

It will not remain in that looped holding pattern forever—and usually not for long. Because once you do this a few times, you find that an absolutely beautiful bonus starts to happen:

- After seeing it come around a few times, you realize it's not as Important or Significant as you once thought, and it never seems to be Urgent enough to do, compared to your other tasks. Since it can always wait, you finally develop the confidence to do what you should've done all along, which is to simply *Eliminate it*.
- Or you will find that somehow the task completely disappears from the Funnel and you don't even think about it until much later. At which point you say to yourself, "I wonder what ever happened with _____." And what you will discover is that *magically* somebody else figured it out, made a decision and solved the problem all on their own. You will be astonished by the resourcefulness and talents of those around you if you give them a chance to figure it out themselves rather than stepping in to do it for them.

Other than that, there are only two other options:

1. It will pass the final checkpoint question when the answer to "Can this wait until later?" turns from yes to no, which we'll deal with in the next chapter. Or . . .
2. It will get "batched."

Batch production is the idea that when you make items in mass groups rather than one at a time, the total cost of each item becomes cheaper. Think of a car . . . it is always going to be cheaper to make and buy an assembly line car from one of the major manu-facturers than it would be to buy a Rolls Royce where each one is individually handmade.

The principle of batching as it relates to *time* was first intro-duced to me when I was a freshman in accounting class at the University of Denver. My professor said, "*Obviously* you don't take a check to the bank the moment you get one from your cli-ent; in small businesses, you typically wait at least a couple days and 'batch' deposit them so as to minimize your trips back and forth to the bank."

The strategy is straightforward: *delaying* the completion of any singular activity so you can maximize the efficiency of perform-ing like activities at the same time. It is *multiplying* your time by waiting to complete similar activities at the same time so as to minimize the cost of *intermittent change* of switching back and forth between activities.

Here are some common activities that are good candidates for batching:

- **E-mail:** You might be nervous about the idea of waiting a few hours to check e-mail because you have the fear that "my customers expect to hear from me *right away!*" No, they don't. That is your fear talking. No reasonable human being expects an immediate response to an e-mail. If they do, then you should fire such customers because they aren't worth your time—literally (see the section in the Eliminate

No reasonable human being expects an immediate response to an e-mail.

chapter on "Unreasonable people"). Besides, I'm not talking about waiting three weeks to get back to your e-mail; I'm talking about waiting a few hours—*very* few things can't wait a couple of hours. Remove *every* single beep, buzz or interruptive alert that you receive when you get a new e-mail. And if possible, move the e-mail icon on your phone off the main screen to one of the side screens. This will allow you to be intentional about when you do check e-mail and prevent you from constantly being sucked into Priority Dilution. By waiting to check e-mails at a few predetermined times of the day, you minimize intermittent change cost, increase your focus and *multiply* your time. Learning to do this won't make you less valuable to your customers; it will make you more valuable.

- **Meeting talk-topics:** A very large number of the e-mails that we get are questions or discussions that *can* wait and would be better handled in a meeting. Particularly if you have regularly scheduled meetings, you should keep a separate running list of "talk topics" for each meeting. Rather than responding to the e-mail, just add the issue to your "talk topics" for the next upcoming meeting. Fewer e-mails *and* more productive meetings—brilliant!

- **Paperwork:** If you're in sales and you're doing proposals or paperwork during peak times of the day and you believe that is the "right time" to be doing them—you are kidding yourself. What you really have is "creative avoidance" and "call reluctance" and you should be overcoming those during that time. Save the paperwork for off-peak hours—or better yet, Delegate it.

- **Any type of shopping:** If you don't yet have a personal assistant or grocery shopper, then keep a running list of what you need and delay as long as possible (POP) your trip to go shopping or to spend time surfing online. That is unless, of course, you get enjoyment out of shopping, but at that point it is a hobby and not a task. It turns out Grandma's grocery list is a really good idea. Not just because it is a list, but because you feel comfortable waiting (Procrastinate) to go to the store; you also minimize (Eliminate) the unnecessary excess time of being there by knowing exactly what you need.
- **Phone calls:** If you have a bunch of phone calls to make, try to group them together one after the other in your day. There is nothing more frustrating than having a call or meeting every other hour for an entire day because you never get dedicated, uninterrupted focus time—which is incredibly rare and valuable these days. Teach your assistant to schedule appointments back to back. It helps keep each of your meetings on time and prevents small pockets of wasted time.
- **Paying bills:** If you don't yet have it Automated (or you don't have the ability) and you don't have a bookkeeper, then pay all your bills at once rather than as they come in one by one. Most people have figured this one out.
- **Thank-you notes:** Unless there is some overarching Urgent consideration, let them pile up for a couple weeks and then write them all out. Your hand will hurt but it saves you intermittent change cost.

There are a million things that you can batch. The key indicator is to pay attention to intermittent change cost: notice when similar insignificant activities are occurring and POP them until you can do them together.

Notice also that as certain activities have been Popped and they cycle back around the Focus Funnel, they will naturally start to group themselves. One task by itself may not ever be Significant enough to cause you to answer the final checkpoint question ("Can this wait until later?") as a no—kicking it down to the final stage. A *group* of activities batched together will, however, because as they build into a larger pile, it matters more to get to them so nothing gets missed. Your e-mail inbox is a prime example of that. While it won't ruin anything to ignore it for a few hours—even for a few days, as I have writing this book—you wouldn't want to leave it for *too* long because then you might miss something Significant.

Trying to keep up with insignificant e-mails one at a time as they come in is an especially horrible investment of your time—because of intermittent change cost. But once there is a pile of e-mails that need to be answered—even if they are all insignificant—the collective power of the whole batch warrants that you deal with them now and that they *cannot* wait until later. At that point they *will* pass the final checkpoint and move down into the final stage of the Focus Funnel: Concentrate.

The pain of patience

Patience is something the world needs more of today. We rush, we rush and we rush some more. We are always trying to find ways of moving faster because of our limited perspective that speed is the premier strategy for advancing our results.

And as the by-product of so many technological advancements, we've now come to expect everything right here and right now. Our urges and desires are catered to, so when we don't get what we want instantly, we become frustrated. We quickly move on to a different provider or a different circumstance that will supply us with the gratification we so urgently desire.

We live in a world that suffers from a severe lack of patience.

By this point I hope you are beginning to see how patience and learning to *Procrastinate on Purpose* can serve as a sound business strategy. Intentionally waiting can help eliminate negative things such as the potential of unnecessary change cost. There is, however, a much greater emotional value to developing the virtue of patience. And it has nothing to do with reducing our costs but rather the strengthening of our character.

On February 6, 2012, at twenty-nine years old, I released my first book, *Take the Stairs*. Within weeks, it reached number one on Amazon, *USA Today* and the *Wall Street Journal*, and number two on the *New York Times* bestseller lists. A few months later, it had already been translated into ten different languages. Ever since, people have asked me how I and our team at Southwestern Consulting suddenly became such a seemingly overnight success.

If only they knew how long we had worked and how long we had been waiting for something big to happen!

The journey began twelve years earlier, when I sat in an auditorium of about a thousand college students. I was going through "sales school," which is the weeklong rock-concert, motivational pep rally, MBA-type training that Southwestern Advantage has put their student dealers through for over a hundred and fifty years. Southwestern Advantage is a sales and leadership program that works with about three thousand college students every year, helping them earn money to pay for college by teaching them how to run their own businesses selling educational reference materials door to door.

The opening speaker was the president of the company, Dan Moore—a Harvard grad who to this day is one of the best speakers I've ever seen. I was seventeen years old, and as I watched him, it occurred to me that one day I would want to do what he did for other people: I wanted to be a speaker. But I knew I would have to wait.

Diligently I worked fourteen hours a day, six days a week, for five summers on straight commission selling books and software door to door in the program. While I was able to rack up nearly $250,000 in profit over those five summers (visit http://swadvan tage.roryvaden.com if you know a college student who you think might enjoy learning about the program), the days of each summer were long and rather challenging. My dream was to leverage that experience into making it as a professional speaker, but for the time being I had to wait.

After finishing graduate school at the University of Denver, I then decided to move on from Southwestern to begin to pursue my dream of becoming a speaker. I was fortunate to be mentored by hall of fame speaker Eric Chester and his good friend and author David Avrin. As part of their guidance, I developed a new dream when they told me to join Toastmasters International. I learned of a contest called the World Championship of Public Speaking, and for two years I dedicated my life to this cause, believing that if I won the world championship, maybe it would give me the credibility I needed to finally achieve my dream. I spoke 304 times for free, received more than three thousand evaluations, spent thousands of hours watching film and thousands of dollars getting coaching. And in 2007, I made it to the world championship as one of the top ten speakers out of over twenty-five thousand contestants . . . and lost. It seemed I had been so close to finally achieving my dream, but it turned out I had to wait.

About that same time, a few partners (including my future wife) and I started our business doing sales training seminars. We were taking our destiny into our own hands by selling tickets to our own live events, and it appeared the dream was finally taking shape. After two and a half years of making dozens of sales calls every day, doing hundreds of workshops and working as hard as ever before, however, we were still losing tens of thousands of dollars in total at the end of each year. With the financial doom of our seminar business hanging in the balance, we turned our focus toward serving our clients through one-on-one sales coaching rather than live events, which meant that once again my dream had to wait.

Having begun to build up a bit more notoriety in the speaking world, I decided that the next step was to write a book. For eighteen months, I approached literary agents and publishers over and over again, to no avail. I was putting everything I had into pursuing my dream; but in what seemed to be a very unfair fate, each plan folded. And it left me . . . waiting.

Then, in November 2010, after the help of numerous people along the way, a whole lot of work and a whole lot of waiting, a literary agent named Nena Madonia took a chance on me. Her contacts opened the door to a publishing deal, and we got the opportunity of a lifetime. Our team at Southwestern Consulting had grown to nearly forty-five people by then and we were ready to take advantage. We spent the next fourteen months waiting for our big moment.

Again with the help and support of many people, we developed and executed a meticulous selling and launch strategy—and the rest is history. But it didn't happen accidentally and it most certainly didn't happen "overnight."

Looking back on my life, I now realize that I wasn't ready for the things I wanted the moment I first decided that I wanted them. And had things gone exactly the way I had them in my mind, then I would've cut myself short on all that I was meant to do.

Had I not made the choice to stay at Southwestern Advantage for as long as I did, enduring the challenge, I may not ever have developed the skills and persistence I needed to achieve what I was able to later. Had I won as a World Champion of Public Speaking for Toastmasters, I may not have ever pursued writing because I probably would've focused on teaching people how to be better speakers. Had we not failed at creating a financially successful seminar division at Southwestern Consulting, we likely would not have the coaching division that now serves as our core business and that has given us a large platform. And had it not been so extremely difficult to get the publishing deal for *Take the Stairs*, we likely wouldn't have put all the time we did into planning such a detailed launch strategy.

Indeed, I can look back on my life and now very clearly see a significant lesson . . .

Sometimes the answer to your dream is "yes." Sometimes it is "no." And sometimes it is "wait."

Sometimes the answer to your dream is "yes." Sometimes it is "no." And sometimes it is "wait."

Time allows for ideas to incubate. Time allows for relationships to develop. Time allows for people to mature. Time is sometimes necessary for our dreams to modify their shape in order to align with the true purpose of our life.

Sometimes time is the very thing that helps you learn to let go of one dream so you can capture another.

Although we can think that now is better, it isn't always. While I strongly believe in a general disposition toward action, one cannot disregard the value of patience. Sometimes patience and allowing for the passage of time is truly the best strategy. Sometimes there is a better plan in place for you that you will discover if you simply wait.

What we learn from the permission of the Incomplete is counterintuitive. It is unnatural. You could even go so far as to say that for many of us it is *uncomfortable.*

And yet there is no limit to the magnitude and significance of understanding the value of *patience* and that *timing* really does matter. While most of us already knew that being too late has a cost, what we have discovered here is that being too early *also* has a cost—and it's one we largely underestimate.

Just as there is great power in the discipline of taking action, there is also great power in the patience of *waiting.*

There are many times when learning to *Procrastinate on Purpose* is necessary and called for.

If you're face to face with someone whom you care about, then that incoming phone call *can wait.*

Just as there is great power in the discipline of taking action, there is also great power in the patience of waiting.

If you're a salesperson and it's your golden prospecting hours, your e-mail *can wait.*

If you're a leader and one of your team members breaks down, your project *can wait.*

If you're an accountant and it's payroll day, organizing your desk *can wait.*

If one of your close family members is dying and this is your last chance to ever see them and tell them you love them, then . . .

It doesn't matter what is going on in your life . . .

What size of a deal you might lose . . .

What customer you might upset . . .

Or how much money it might cost . . .

Everything else can wait!

Because in business, what you don't get done today can likely be done tomorrow, but with family, what doesn't get done today is gone forever.

The good news is that when you know how to *multiply* your time, you will never have to choose between one and the other at the same time . . .

Chapter Summary

Procrastinate: The Permission of Incomplete

KEY POINTS

- Timing matters. Just as there is great power in the discipline of acting, there is also great power in the patience of *waiting*.
- Waiting to do something when "we know it is something that we *should* do but we don't really want to do it" is Procrastination. Waiting because "we are deciding that *now* is not the *right* time" is Patience.
- Inaction that results from indulgence is Procrastination. Inaction that results from intention is Patience. *Procrastinate on Purpose* is a synonym for Patience.
- Gun Slingers have no problem waiting until the last minute. They have to beware of waiting too long and causing "after last-minute costs." Worry Warts need to practice patience so as not to incur unexpected change cost. You need both to have a great team.
- Worry Warts typically carry the weight of the world and they feel pressure to do everything and to do it *now*. They need to give themselves the permission of Incomplete and to learn to be okay with things just being okay. It is okay to slow down.

UNEXPECTED FINDINGS

- Waiting till the last minute is good because it reduces your vulnerability to unexpected change cost. Waiting until *after* the last minute is bad because it creates stress, anxiety and many negative actual costs to a business. So you don't want to be late, but you also don't want to be too early; Multipliers work to be precisely on time.

- Doing something early is not the same as *creating* more time. It is just taking time from tomorrow and moving it into today and adding the risk of unexpected change cost.

- Patience isn't just waiting. It is also giving yourself time to breathe. It is creating margin in your life. And it is freeing yourself from the fear that you're not good enough so you must do everything now in order to prove that you are.

STARTLING STATISTICS

- Ninety-one percent of people have a general belief that things will work out for the best.

ACTION QUESTIONS

- In what areas of your life do you need to learn to be okay with things being just okay and to trust that time will help sort things out?

8

Concentrate

The Permission to Protect

F armers have a harvest each and every year. It's one period of the year when all their crops must be taken up at just the right time in order for their survival. Do you know how many hours the average farmer works per day during harvest season? About eighteen.

They usually wake up around four thirty a.m. and come in at about eleven p.m. Given the fact that their entire livelihood and well-being over the next year depends on the fruits of this harvest season, do you think that being sick is an option for a farmer during harvest?

Do you think that being tired is an option for the farmer? Do you think that taking time off to "evaluate other career options" is a possibility for a farmer during harvest?

Absolutely not. There is a short window of opportunity when the harvest must be captured. It doesn't matter if the farmer would rather work eighteen hours a day at some other time of the year, because the harvest is when the harvest is.

Feeling fatigued, burnt out or dissatisfied doesn't even enter into a farmer's decision-making framework during the harvest because that is the only time of the year that will produce the type of results needed to make life work.

Regardless of how the farmer is feeling during the harvest, he instead sets up his thinking in a way that allows him to maximize the reap. Whether or not you've ever stepped foot on a farm, you need to become intimately acquainted with the philosophy of a farmer:

During the harvest, you work double-time part time so that later you can have full-time free time.

During the harvest, you work double-time part time so that later you can have full-time free time.

Why are we talking about farming?

Farmers have relentless focus, uncompromised commitment and an almost radical addiction to completing the task at hand—which is exactly what you need when the time comes to apply the final permission and choice of a Multiplier: Concentrate.

The word "concentrate" is the perfect word to use here for a few reasons. Concentrate is a verb that instructs us "to bring all efforts, faculties, activities, etc., to bear on one thing or activity."* Concentrate, as a verb, is exactly what you need to do when you get to this point in the Focus Funnel.

The most powerful reason we chose this term, however, is because of its use as a noun. Concentrate, as a noun, is "an intense form of something," such as juice concentrate. Incidentally, concentrate is

---

*Dictionary.com, "concentrate," dictionary.reference.com/browse/concentrate?s-t.

also the opposite of dilution. As in, it is the antithesis of Priority Dilution—the very problem this book is intended to address.

The concept of "concentrate" (noun) is an acute representation of how a Multiplier thinks. A Multiplier's mind is perpetually working very quickly to calculate and recalculate which activities are going to have the most Significant long-term impact. In the early twentieth century, an Italian economist named Vilfredo Pareto developed a theory that has since evolved into the 80-20 Rule—that 20 percent of efforts result in 80 percent of results, that the top 20 percent of sellers produce 80 percent of sales, and so on. Like a highly magnified version of this 80-20 Rule, the gift of Multipliers is to immediately identify what use of their time is going to have the most impact. That is, what activities can they spend time on today that will create more time tomorrow?

Then they immediately home in with uncanny focus on whatever activity that is. In other words, they concentrate on the most concentrated use of their time. And Multipliers use tools to help them Concentrate because they know the damage distraction can cause. It should be no surprise, then, that while only 8 percent of all people consistently use a written detailed schedule of how to spend their time in a week, we estimate that about 85 percent of the Multipliers we surveyed use one.*

Even more striking is that, contrary to our original hypothesis that Multipliers would have sophisticated systems for handling e-mail that we hoped we could share with readers, they didn't have any answers for us about how to better use e-mail. In fact, virtually

---

*Focused 40 Survey conducted by Southwestern Consulting 2012–2013.

every single Multiplier that we talked to cited e-mail as something that has drastically reduced their effectiveness. As one of the Multipliers I came across commented, "I hate e-mail because it has detracted from my natural ability to identify what matters most. My inbox has become nothing other than a way to organize other people's priorities."

> *My inbox has become nothing other than a way to organize other people's priorities.*

The Focus Funnel, then, like a written schedule, is meant to be a tool we can use to help make sure we are not getting distracted by insignificant things. At each stage, the Funnel has presented us with a checkpoint question to make sure that we are on track.

In the Eliminate stage, it was, "Is this task something I can live without?"

In the Automate stage, it was, "Can this task be systematized?"

In the Delegate stage, it was, "Can this task be performed by someone else?"

In the Procrastinate stage, it was, "Can this wait until later?"

If the answer to each of the previous four questions is no, then—and only then—you finally have something that is a *priority*.

You can have a great conviction.

You now *know* the timing is right.

At this point it is time to *act*.

It is time to pull the trigger.

It is time to focus on progress, not perfection.

It is time to "Ready, aim, fire."

It is time to *Take the Stairs*.

It is time to *Concentrate*.

It is time to do that very thing that you *know* you should be doing. And now you know for *sure* that it is precisely the thing you should be doing at that moment.

A priority is the *next most Significant* thing on your list. And so a priority becomes any task that rises to such a level of Significance that it is beyond the convenience of what your schedule allows.

In other words, the *Procrastinate on Purpose* system of multiplying your time is not so much about identifying what your "priori*ties*" are. We already know that your "priorities" are something like: Faith, Family, Fitness, Fun, Faculty and Finances.

The real question is what is your priori*ty*?—singular!

As in, what is *the next*—and only—priority?

You can't really have multiple priorities. By virtue of the definition of the word "priority," it means "that which is in front of all others." So, you can only have one priority—and it's always the very thing that you are doing right now!

> You can't really have
> multiple priorities.

Whatever you are choosing to spend your time doing at any given moment is your priority—at that moment. And it should be! That's called "being present." This idea alone may help you enhance your focus by allowing yourself to be completely absorbed in what is happening in front of you at any given moment rather than being "off someplace else in your mind," where you are thinking about something else but you can't take action on it because your body is where you are right now.

So POP whatever it is in your mind and be where you are right now. And if the thing you are doing now is *not* what you really want your priority to be, then Eliminate that thing in front of you, Automate it, Delegate it, Procrastinate it or Complete it as fast as possible and sprint over to the thing you know you should be doing!

But do not lie to yourself and say that even though you are doing one thing, your priority is really another.

You might have more Significant things you *want* to be doing, but any time that you are not doing them, they are not *truly* your priority.

That is one of the great deceptions of this life. In our minds, we *think* that our priority is our family, or our priority is being successful, or our priority is our faith, but if that isn't what we are *actually doing*, then it isn't our priority!

If you are watching TV, then you are choosing that as your priority.

If you are standing in line for coffee, then you are choosing that as your priority.

If you are playing games on your phone . . .

If you are driving to work . . .

If you are answering e-mail . . .

If you are exercising . . .

If you are reading this book . . .

Then that is your priority.

Some priorities *are* vehicles to get to other ones. For example, driving to work may be your priority for some period every day because it is a *necessary* step to get you to the physical location you need to be in, in order to achieve your goal of being successful at work so that you can make enough money so that you can take care of your kids.

That's fine.

Remember the core message of this book: "You multiply your time by giving yourself permission to spend time on things today that create more time tomorrow."

You aren't choosing to spend time on them today because they are the end goal.

You aren't choosing to spend time on them today because they are the most convenient.

You aren't choosing to spend time on them because someone else wants you to.

You are selecting these activities because of one and only one property that they have—that they will likely create better results and more time for you tomorrow.

It's good to know that one current priority is a step to take you to the next one.

It will bring you a lot of clarity to know *why* you are doing everything that you are doing. It will create a connected *purpose* to *everything* you are doing.

And not only that, but it will help you realize all the things you are doing that are *not* taking you where you really want to go. It will help you see all the things you are doing that are *not* helping you create the results you want in your life. Those things will become more and more obvious to you, and once you get to that point, you will most likely have another powerful insight:

> *Until you accomplish your next most Significant priority,* everything else *is a distraction.*

Until you accomplish your next most Significant priority, *everything else* is a distraction.

That brings us to the critical question you have to always be asking yourself: *"Is what I'm doing right now the next most Significant use of my time?"*

Is it the thing that is moving you toward creating the best results? Is it the thing that is moving you toward making your greatest contribution? Is it the thing that is moving you toward making the impact you want to make?

Is it the thing that is making the most out of the available time that you have? Is it the thing that is enabling you at that moment to be your *highest* self?

If not, then it is a distraction. It is a temptation. It is a pressure. It is someone else's priority and not your own. It could be a million things, but what it definitely is *not* is your priority.

And if that is the case, stop whatever it is you are doing in that moment and get the heck out of there!

Get back to what you should be doing. Get back on track. Get realigned with what you know your priority should be.

But most of us don't . . .

Most of us continue doing things that we know are not moving us down the path we know we should be following.

We continue going through a bunch of motions that are insignificant.

We keep doing the same mindless things over and over and over again.

Why?

Is it because we don't care about using our life for the purpose it was intended? Is it because we don't value our time?

No, actually it's just the opposite.

What we have done is traded the things we know we should be doing for the things that other people want us to do.

We have allowed ourselves to be commanded by the Tyranny of the Urgent into things that are not Significant, but they are in front of us.

We have given in to the pressure of the incredible volume and noise of all the busy work simply because . . .

We have a big fat fear of letting other people down.

We don't want people to think we don't care about them, so we make ourselves available 24/7 to answer their beck and call.

We don't want to be seen as mean, so we agree to things that aren't right for us.

We don't want to be considered resistant, so we go along with decisions that we know are the wrong ones at the wrong time.

We don't want to be viewed as disloyal, so we overcommit.

We don't want to be thought of as weak, so we take on too much.

We don't want people to think we're selfish, so we ignore our priority and focus on theirs.

And all the while, the thing we are missing is the permission to Protect.

The fifth permission

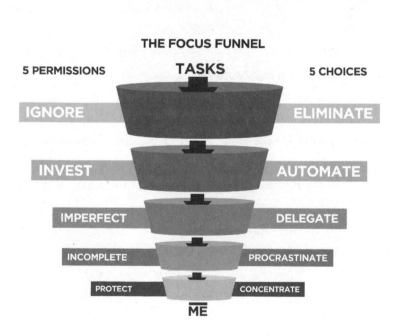

THE FOCUS FUNNEL

5 PERMISSIONS — TASKS — 5 CHOICES

IGNORE — ELIMINATE

INVEST — AUTOMATE

IMPERFECT — DELEGATE

INCOMPLETE — PROCRASTINATE

PROTECT — CONCENTRATE

ME

We haven't given ourselves the permission to focus on our priority instead of theirs.

We haven't believed in ourselves enough to zero in on what is going to have the most Significant impact rather than the one that is just going to have the most immediate impact.

We haven't given ourselves the confidence to trust in what we know is the *right* thing.

Because in our never-ending journey for approval and in our pride point of always wanting to serve others, we missed something truly Significant:

Your highest obligation to other people is to be your highest self.

Your highest obligation to other people is to be your highest self.

"If there is a loss of cabin pressure, put *your* mask on first *then* assist those around you."

You have to give yourself the permission to focus on and protect: *you.*

Not because you are a jerk, but because you care.

Not because you're selfish, but because you aim to serve others.

Not because it's the best thing for you, but because it is the best thing for those around you.

You were put here on earth to do something that no one else can do. It is yours and yours alone to complete. It requires you to be your highest self and if you don't do that thing, you are going to inhibit those around you from doing theirs.

As a Multiplier, it is your obligation to spend time on things today that create more opportunity for those around you tomorrow.

It is to do the things that are right, not only for now, but for the future.

And if you haven't trusted yourself before, then I hope you see the reason it matters now. And I hope the Focus Funnel will give you the confidence and conviction to help you determine what your next priority is—and what it should be. I hope it will help you give yourself the permission to Protect it.

The permission to Protect yields a straightforward and pragmatic strategy for you to incorporate into your life today, which is to:

Temporarily ignore the small stuff so that you can Concentrate on the big stuff.

So the *only* way you can let others down . . .

The *only* way you do a disservice to those around you . . .

> *Temporarily ignore the small stuff so that you can Concentrate on the big stuff.*

The *only* way you can't appropriately pay back everyone who has helped you become who you are . . .

Is to trade the Significant things that you are supposed to do for insignificant ones.

TRADING 15-MINUTE POCKETS

MULTIPLIER MINDSET CASE STUDY

Tonya Mayer, Direct Sales, Rodan + Fields
Nashville, Tennessee

Mother of four boys, eight years previously a teacher, and with a number one priority of leading a Christian life, Tonya Mayer says that her massive success is a by-product of focusing on serving and sharing more than it is focusing on selling. Make no mistake about it, though, the woman can sell—and lead! In just four and a half years, she has grown a team from scratch to fourteen hundred people and has become one of the top independent consultants with a home-based business for Rodan + Fields.

"When I first started this business, I didn't know if it would really be possible to fit it in with everything else I had going on. At the time I joined Rodan + Fields, I had a two-year-old, a four-year-old, a first grader and a fourth grader! I sometimes struggled with the guilt of feeling like I had to let other things go." Tonya talks with such a bright glow and warm smile that you can't help but feel compelled to interrupt her with a giant bear hug.

"I remember one time when a good friend had called me who also had a child at my son's school to ask me what I was doing. I said, 'I'm frantically making eighty cupcakes because I just found out they are having a party tomorrow in class!' When I asked her what she was making, she said 'I'm bringing in flavored water.' I told her, 'Wow, I wish I would've done that' and she said something that really stuck with me: 'You know, Tonya, you don't always have to be a cupcake mom; it really is okay to be a water mom once in a while.'

You don't always have to be a cupcake mom; it really is okay to be a water mom once in a while.

"Around that time I figured out that we are always trading one thing for another. In my case, I was trading my time for a *feeling* of being a good mom. Sometimes it is those little things that matter, but for the most part I realized that insignificant things like 'making cupcakes' is not what makes me a good mom. Then I made a decision that there are probably other things that I could *trade* to accomplish some of the things that I wanted without taking away from my family, my health or my relationship with God. Now it is rare that you will see me looking at a magazine or watching TV, and I gave up my book club and instead started listening to books when I'm in the car.

"Once I started to be intentional about every moment of my day, I discovered that it is amazing how many little fifteen-minute intervals we waste throughout the day. It might be waiting for an appointment to show up, standing in line or commuting in the car. My focus switched to 'How can I make these fifteen-minute pockets valuable to my life and business?' Looking back now, I can see how significant all that time adds up to be and that a big part of our team philosophy has been learning to build your business in fifteen-minute increments.

"Most of the people who start in our business already have a full-time job, and if I asked them if they had ten to fifteen extra hours in their week to put into something like this, they'd say, 'No way.' But when I ask people if they can make two or three phone calls in a few of those fifteen-minute 'pockets' throughout the day, they say, 'Of course! No problem.' Once you get past the belief barrier that 'I'm too busy' and you learn to completely focus in and concentrate for even just fifteen minutes at a time, you'll see that you can build a huge business that way. Now we even do a lot of our training in fifteen-minute station rotation small groups. And I answer e-mail in four fifteen-minute pockets each day."

I ask Tonya, "How do you get yourself to quickly focus in these short bursts of time?"

She replies, "I know this is silly but I make these little deals with myself all day long. 'If I make these three phone calls, then I can have _____.' Or 'Once I accomplish (insert any small goal), then I get to do _____.'"

Intrigued about this light and playful system, I ask, "So fifteen minutes at a time isn't very long. How do you choose what to spend the time on?"

"At this point for me, it's pretty simple. I've determined that the most impactful thing I can be doing is training up my leaders and personally recruiting to lead by example. Those are the two main activities that are going to help my team grow. Training and coaching leaders is first and foremost because I can't lead thousands of people and give them all everything they need, so I want to take the people who are closest to me and work hard at transferring skills to these future leaders. I want to lock arms with them to make sure they become the leaders of their teams.

"Spending my time with potential leaders is a priority and it is a joy in my life that I really draw fulfillment from. The people who have shared their goals with me and are willing to do the work are the ones who are easiest to develop into leaders. They have become people I do life with and have fun with outside of work. I adore the people on my team! They are amazing.

"If anyone comes to me for help—leader or not—then I will make it a priority to help get them going because I want to see them succeed. As long as they are following through on what they can control and doing the things they commit to, then I'll never stop believing in them. Sometimes people want the success but they aren't willing to do the work, and I realized that for this relationship to flourish, we each must be willing to do our part. Otherwise I'm trading my time that could be spent with those willing to work, for someone who isn't really up for the journey.

"Most of all, I've realized that each second I'm procrastinating, or not doing what I'm supposed to be doing, or I'm distracted, or I'm not investing my time in the greatest way possible, is one more second that is being taken away from the time I get to spend with my family—and that is just not something I'm willing to trade."

Your next most significant thing

There are times when you need to wait, there are times when you need to *Procrastinate on Purpose* and there are times when patience is the answer . . . but it is not now. Once a task passes through all the checkpoints of the Focus Funnel, you can have confidence that it is the right thing for you to do and that it must be done at this moment.

Your job is simply to do the *next most Significant thing* and not to worry about anything else. You don't have to worry about everything you have to do. You only have to focus on taking the *next step.* Success is simply a series of completing the next most significant priority.

This is where you cannot wait any longer. This is when you have to take charge of your own destiny. This is when you have to realize that nobody else is going to do it for you and so you have to do it now.

Because there is no such thing as an overnight success.

There is no such thing as unintentionally being discovered.

There is no such thing as a random happenstance of your dreams coming true.

Excellence is *never* an accident. It is *always* the result of work, and faith, and fight and discipline and action.

Your dream matters too much to lose to distraction.

Your dream matters too much to be comfortable.

Your dream matters too much to give up out of courtesy.

Your dream matters too much to lose to fear.

Your dream matters too much to be ignored.

Your dream matters so much that the next step has to be protected!

If something is the next most Significant thing related to your dream, you have to Protect it, you have to do it, and you have to do it now!

Until you do, everything else is a distraction.

So you have to work.

You have to fight.

You have to hustle.

You have to persist.

You have to act.

You have to concentrate.

Chapter Summary

Concentrate: The Permission to Protect

KEY POINTS

- Work double-time part-time now so that later you can have full-time free time.

- A priority is any task that rises to such a level of Significance that it is beyond the convenience of what your schedule allows. You force it to be the first focus.

- Until you accomplish your next most Significant priority, *everything else* in life is a distraction.

- The Focus Funnel is a tool to help ensure that—as much as possible—you're always spending your time on your next most Significant thing. The critical question you have to always be asking yourself is: "Is what I'm doing right now the next most Significant use of my time?"

- Once a task passes through all the checkpoints of the Focus Funnel, you can have confidence that it is the right thing for you to do and that it must be done at that moment.

- Temporarily ignore the small stuff so that you can Concentrate on the big stuff.

UNEXPECTED FINDINGS

- We have a very emotional fear of letting other people down that causes us to sacrifice our priorities for other people's.

- "Concentrate" serves both as a great verb to remind us to take action and also as a meaningful noun that represents the skill of quickly identifying what the next most Significant step will be.

- Your highest obligation to other people is to be your highest self.
- Most Multipliers have a general distaste for e-mail and view it as a way of "organizing other people's priorities" rather than as a tool to help them focus on what is Significant.
- As a Multiplier, it is your obligation to spend time on things today that create more opportunity for those around you tomorrow.

STARTLING STATISTICS

- Only 8 percent of people consistently use a written detailed schedule of how to spend their time in a week. Incidentally, that is about the same percentage of the population that we estimate are true Multipliers. Our inference is that Multipliers allow their schedule and their calculations of priorities to proactively dictate how they spend their time rather than allowing their inbox to reactively dictate how they spend their time.

ACTION QUESTIONS

- What do you need to give yourself permission to concentrate on? How would concentrating on that create more opportunity for those around you?

Part 3

The Next Step

9

Multiplying
Your Results

n *Take the Stairs,* we shared some research from a survey of ten thousand employees who were asked the question "In a given forty-hour workweek, how much time do you spend on non-job-related tasks?" The average person admitted to wasting 2.09 hours . . .

Each day!

And according to the U.S. Bureau of Labor Statistics, the average salaried employee in the United States at that time was making $39,795 a year, or $19.13 per hour.

Which means that our procrastination costs employers $10,396 per year . . .

Per employee.

Thus, one of the most popular catchphrases from *Take the Stairs* has been that "procrastination is the most expensive invisible cost in business today."

And I still believe that is true because procrastination affects every person, in every company, every day. (If you go to my blog at roryvadenblog.com, you'll see that we created a "Procrastination Cost Calculator" so that you can put in the actual numbers of your team members and their average earnings, to calculate how much procrastination is costing you or your team.)

In our consulting work with clients over the last few years, however—and in trying to apply our own practices to our own company at Southwestern Consulting—we've become tuned in to even *more* invisible costs.

For example, another analysis we do with our consulting clients as part of our initial research phase is a "Salesperson Cost of Acquisition Calculator."

It is a series of questions that we ask clients about how much time and money they spend in all the different phases of marketing, recruiting, hiring, on-boarding and training just one single salesperson.

For anything that is an activity that takes someone's time from his or her organization—like conducting an interview—we simply do an M.V.O.T. (money value of time, from Delegate, in chapter six) breakdown of what that person's time is empirically *worth*. Thus, we are pretty easily able to convert that time into money and add it to the other *real* costs the organization has, like production costs, advertising and so on.

We almost never find that the cost of recruiting, training and hiring just *one* salesperson is less than fifteen thousand dollars, and we've seen it be as high as eighty thousand. And just think that some companies are turning over 30 to 80 percent of their sales force every year! So you can imagine their excitement when we can show them how to recruit better salespeople, faster—*and* get them productively closing business in much less time.

Procrastination and employee turnover, then, are both examples of "invisible costs." There are other "invisible costs" to your organization, though, aren't there?

On the one hand, you have the cost of turnover and all the money that you lose when someone leaves your company with all that you've invested in them. But on the other hand, what is the cost of hanging on to people too long? That can be one of the greatest costs of all because it eats away at the fabric of your team and can destroy your culture.

I remember one of the first, best—and still to this day toughest—decisions that I ever made as a leader was to get rid of a bad apple.

Hiring and firing alone is a perfect application of multiplying your time because some people create more time and results for your organization tomorrow, while others cost you more time and money tomorrow.

Think about the cost of gossip and interoffice, interpersonal conflict and relational dynamics. How much time do you spend on that? I'm guessing a lot.

And what about all the time spent switching back and forth unnecessarily between tasks? What if you added up all that time of people who were falsely thinking they were multitasking?

Why am I talking about all of this?

Well, because what do all of these have in common?

- The Cost of Procrastination
- The Cost of Turnover
- The Cost of Indecision
- The Cost of Interpersonal Conflict and
- Intermittent Change Cost

They are all *time* costs.

And yet the vast majority of companies don't often think of these as *real* costs simply because they don't measure them.

But they *are* real costs. They are *very* real costs.

If there is anything we've seen over and over in this book, it is that *time* is worth *more* than money.

Yet almost no leaders *think* and *act* and make *decisions* that way.

Think about it like this . . .

Do you think any big company goes through the year without making a revenue budget? Of course not.

Do you think any big company goes through the year without tracking expenses? Of course not.

Do you think any big company goes through the year without producing a set of financial statements? Of course not.

How many hours are spent in meetings poring over financial statements, going line by line through the Profit and Loss, worrying about cutting every little penny wherever they possibly can? Thousands.

A big company would *never* operate without a financial review.

But when was the last time you ever heard of a company getting their top people together to focus their energy specifically on the question "What is currently sucking up the most unnecessary use of our *time*?"

Never!

We search and scour with a fine-tooth comb, racking our brain for every possible solution, to find any way we can to save a few dollars.

Meanwhile . . .

We completely ignore the gigantic gaping cavernous pit that is all of the ways our teams—and we—are wasting *time*.

As individuals, we regularly think about how we can be more efficient—sure. But as teams, companies and organizations, we *never* talk about all the things we are doing that are a complete waste of time.

You are looking in the wrong places and you are asking the wrong questions!

The most *Significant* opportunity for cost savings in most companies today is not saving *money*. It's saving *time*.

Your most expensive costs will never be the *dollars* you spend; they will be the *time* you spend.

You can get dollars back but you can never get *time* back.

> *The most* Significant *opportunity for cost savings in most companies today is not saving* money. *It's saving* time.

If you want to *multiply* your profitability as a company, don't *just* ask the question "Where can we save *money*?"

Instead put your best and most creative minds on the question "Where are our best opportunities to save *time*?"

Just like you have a *financial* review, every so often you need a *time* review. Consulting with companies and teams about how to apply the Focus Funnel to their entire organization has become a critical part of what we now do at Southwestern Consulting. One reason why we get brought in as an outside pair of eyes is because for many of us who are operating under the same paradigm as we've always been, the most obvious places to save time can be the ones that are also the most elusive.

Creating a POP culture

I hope you can now see the power in being more intentional about your strategies for how to use your time. While you can surely save a few hundred dollars on "getting your paper clips from a different vendor"—and you should—it is even more important to think about how you could save millions of dollars by *multiplying* your time throughout your entire organization.

Imagine if every single person in your organization, team or family were a Multiplier.

What if each person on the team was doing exactly *his or her* next most Significant thing at precisely the best time?

What if you reduced the amount of time being spent on insignificant activities?

What if you completely got rid of everything that didn't need to be done in the first place?

What if you used a system like Infusionsoft that automated everything that was happening over and over again?

What if every task was delegated to the perfect person with just the precise skill set and the appropriate decision-making ability to handle the challenge at hand?

What if your entire team had the perfect mix of patience and action?

What would that look like for you? Can you even imagine how big, awesome, fun and profitable that would be? What kind of impact on the world that would be?

You would truly be *multiplying*.

That would be what we call a *Procrastinate on Purpose* culture—or a POP culture for short.

How do you do that? Well, pretty simple, really.

First, you take all the principles of this book that we've gone through and you apply them to your own life. You lead by example and you show people by experimenting with the application of what we hope you've learned thus far.

Then, you teach these principles to everyone in your organization.

As a review, an individual Multiplier looks like this:

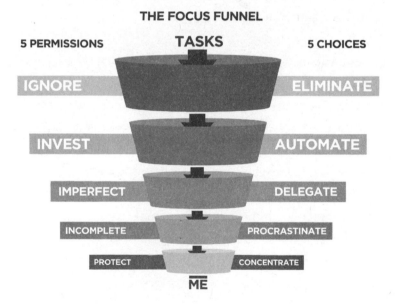

THE FOCUS FUNNEL

5 PERMISSIONS	TASKS	5 CHOICES
IGNORE		ELIMINATE
INVEST		AUTOMATE
IMPERFECT		DELEGATE
INCOMPLETE		PROCRASTINATE
PROTECT		CONCENTRATE
	ME	

You teach your team about the distinctions between:

- **One-dimensional thinking:** "Managing your time" by doing things fast and efficiently in order to try to squeeze more into whatever time you have available. This is like running.

- **Two-dimensional thinking:** "Prioritizing your time" by the Urgent and Important grid to borrow time from one area of your life to focus instead on another. It's the skill of putting one thing in front of the others. This is like juggling.
- **Three-dimensional thinking:** "Multiplying your time" by adding in the calculation of Significance. And to specifically give yourself the emotional *permission* to spend time on those things today that will create more time tomorrow. This is like planting seeds.

Next, you teach everyone how to process all of their incoming "stuff" by using the Focus Funnel to help decide how to process each task that comes their way. Make sure they know that the ultimate litmus test is to, whenever possible, spend time on things today that create more time tomorrow.

You will of course need to teach them how to access the five *Permissions*, since choosing how to spend your time is no longer about calendars and checklists, tasks and To Do lists because time management isn't just logical—it's emotional.

And you are going to want your leaders to understand all of the different types of *costs* we've discussed:

- Actual cost (the five-dollar coffee)
- Opportunity cost (what you're not able to buy as a result of spending five dollars on the coffee)
- Hidden cost (the potential forty-five dollars in interest lost by choosing to spend that five dollars rather than invest it)

- Money value of time, or M.V.O.T., cost (the hourly rate of a person's time spent on any activity)
- Unnecessary change cost (the cost of rework)
- Intermittent change cost (the cost of time lost as the result of changing back and forth unnecessarily between multiple activities)
- Invisible cost (a combination of real costs and M.V.O.T. costs that simply go unmeasured and unmonitored in an organization)

You will also want to teach your leaders that the greatest potential for cost savings in the organization may not be by reducing financial expenses but that it very well likely could be by reducing time expenditures.

In other words, you are going to set up your entire corporate structure in a way that works to:

1. **Eliminate** unnecessary initiatives, meaningless activity, useless bureaucracy, the wrong people, unproductive meetings and obstacles that are holding your team back.
2. **Automate** regimented tasks, necessary but monotonous work and mechanisms that help reduce "think time" on tasks that are noncreative.
3. **Delegate** work and decision-making authority to the specialized talent you have on your team. As my friend and Multiplier Steve Savage says, "Drive decision making downward." Purposely enable the vast majority of decisions to be

Drive decision making downward.

heavily influenced and, hopefully, made by the people who are closest to the front lines.

4. **Procrastinate** on projects that aren't yet at the "right time" for your organization or anything you aren't sure is critical to the future direction of the team.

5. **Concentrate** on the next most Significant step for yourself and your organization. Try to create a culture where every task and decision finds the person who is perfectly appropriate for the condition.

All throughout the entire organization, you are going to promote and reinforce the thinking that everyone make the Significance calculation. You will also encourage them to do the things today that create more time and results tomorrow. If you give them the permission to do that, you will be astounded to find that they have incredible ideas about exactly what needs to be done.

At the same time, work to incorporate a *Take the Stairs* mindset of getting people excited about doing the things they know they should be doing even when they don't feel like doing them. Champion the reduction of multitasking and intermittent change cost through the power of focus and encouraging people to Concentrate.

Of course it will be rather challenging to ensure that all of this happens. While you are doing all of that for the organization, you also have to keep up with your own life and work. We hope you'll be using all that you've learned to do your best at appropriately finding the patience to wait and the discipline to act.

It may seem daunting to transform an entire culture, but it's worth it. There is nothing more exciting than being in a culture where *everyone* is *multiplying* their time and the value of the organization by spending time on things today that create more time and results tomorrow.

You might think that it's "easier said than done"—and that is for sure—but if you are working to transform a culture, you have one asset that you should never underestimate: people.

INFLUENCE THINKING

MULTIPLIER MINDSET CASE STUDY

Steve Adams, Custom Clothier, Tom James

Austin, Texas

Steve Adams is a divisional president and has worked with the Tom James clothing company for over twenty-four years. Tom James is the world's largest manufacturer and retailer of custom clothing. It has more than three thousand employees worldwide and provides the finest clothing to business executives.

As one of the few remaining vertically integrated clothing retailers (meaning they control the entire manufacturing process "from sheep to suit"), Tom James offers unparalleled value to those with an eye for quality. Clothes range from a six-hundred-dollar fully custom entry-level suit to 100 percent handmade Oxxford using Holland & Sherry cloth.

Their haberdashers (who also function as their sales force) come directly to your home or office, so you never wait in line, fight for parking or covet a garment that doesn't come in your size. And because they don't advertise or operate brick-and-mortar stores, they pass those savings along to customers.

Humble and subdued (he says that his title "divisional president" is a fancy way of saying he gets to take credit for other people's success), Steve is one of the most effective "quiet leaders" on the planet. A true student of the game with a genuine heart of service, he has expanded his team across international borders with steady, consistent growth. He believes that his entire job as a leader can be boiled down to one simple task: to influence people's thinking. Having not always been as successful as he is today, he developed this philosophy when he realized that the first person's thinking that needed influencing was his own.

"In April of 2005, I had been with Tom James for fifteen years and I had only managed to recruit one person into my organization that hadn't left. I was coming off a month where I sold twenty-six units, which some of our top salespeople do in a day. I was exhausted with Tom James and I blamed the company for how tired I was. I blamed it for my financial ruin. And I blamed it for my overall lack of success as a leader.

"I decided to take another job but I actually called a meeting with some of the senior executives at Tom James so that I could give them a piece of my mind before I left the company. I'd set it up so that I could tell them how pathetic they were and so I could finally take a few parting shots at them on my way out.

"The meeting was in Houston and I lived in Austin, and I was too broke to fly, so I drove. During the course of that drive, I reflected on my career and the fifteen people I had hired of which fourteen had quit. I reflected on all the different leaders I had been transferred to at my request. I thought about all the different sales territories I had been given because I had convinced people there was something wrong with the one I had.

"On that fateful drive it finally occurred to me that the only thing that all of those situations had in common ... was me. The worst part was that for fifteen years I had been quoting all of the success principles to everyone around me but my life didn't reflect a single one of them. I *finally*, once and for all, accepted responsibility, and by the time I got to Houston, I had a sixty-second meeting with them where I apologized for wasting their time and I turned around and drove right back home.

"Rather than quitting the company, I resolved that I was going to stay and shape my thinking in a way that I would take accountability for *everything*. If a Scud missile hit my house, it was going to be my fault for moving there. I decided that I was going to force my thinking to be about what I was grateful for rather than about what things I did not have. I chose a leadership strategy that focused on helping influence the thinking of the people around me in directions that were positive for their own lives—and everything radically changed.

"Around that time, I was privileged to be mentored by several great people, including Todd Browne, Dave Wykle and our CEO of more than thirty years, Jim McEachern. They helped shape my thinking in that not only was I supposed to set a good example in sales, but also to influence the *thinking* of the people around me with the timeless principles that will help them become a success. They also taught me to spend my time with things and people that I really can *influence* and to let go of things I cannot control.

"Some people have a high disposition for making their biggest impact through lots of customers—they are sales leaders. Other people have a higher predisposition for multiplying their influence through other team members— they are team leaders. What really matters is accepting accountability for your results and determining how you can make the most lasting and significant impact.

"Through Jim McEachern and other leaders in our company, I was just so lucky because they changed the trajectory of my entire life—they influenced my thinking. Now I hope to do that for the people I work with. Making that kind of difference in the world is tough to do with the limited time we all have, which is why I'll never forget something that Jim told me toward the end of his life as he was battling cancer. He said, 'If I could do it all over again, I would find those who really wanted to lead other people and I would have spent more time with them. I would've invested more time with fewer people.'"

I would've invested more time with fewer people.

Patience and action

Throughout this book we've looked at the significance of the dichotomy between patience and action.

You need both of them.

You need fast and slow.

You need now and later.

You need *Procrastinate on Purpose* to give you the patience to wait.

And you need *Take the Stairs* to give you the discipline to act.

This book is meant to give you a series of tools to enhance your thinking so that you can follow a decision-making process similar to that used by some of the most successful people on the planet: the Multipliers.

What Multipliers understand better than everyone else, though, is that while the thinking is critically important, it is ultimately the *acting* that is monumental.

You have to act.

You have to do.

You have to try.

You can work while you wait.

You can do everything in your power today to make your dream come true *and* at the same time trust that if it doesn't, it is because the wait is preparing you for the day that it will.

But you must work now.

You must do whatever it is that you know you can do.

You must take the next step.

And regardless of whether you encounter failure or success, you must continue to act.

There will likely be times when the things in this book don't work out like you hoped.

And after that, you will still have to act.

You will still have to do.

You will still have to keep going.

There will be other times when the things in this book really *do* work for you.

And after that, you're still going to have to work.

You're still going to have to fight.

And that is because of one *timeless* truth, which we've said at Southwestern for years:

> *Success is never owned; it is only rented—and the rent is due every day.*

Success is never owned; it is only rented—and the rent is due every day.

Which is basically where this book ends and *Take the Stairs* begins.

But one last thing before we go . . .

Seed Planters and Fire Fighters

Being a "Seed Planter" is the best image I can conjure up for what a Multiplier would look like in nature.

Planting "seeds" is not something you would necessarily do for short-term satisfaction but rather for long-term satisfaction. That is the difference between Urgency and Significance.

A "Fire Fighter," though, is focused on the immediate task at hand—which sometimes is a matter of life and death. One of my best friends is a Fire Fighter and there is no doubt about the

Importance, the Urgency and the Significance that real fire fighters have in the real world.

Metaphorically speaking, there will still be times that you will need to be a Fire Fighter. It's not as if things won't come up that require you to drop what you are doing and make that your priority. In those moments you will find, however, that this methodology is validated, as the task at hand will rank high in all three categories of Importance, Urgency and Significance.

So, as with many of the concepts we've uncovered, the goal is not to be always one or the other, but to appropriately be both.

I make no apologies whatsoever, though, that one of my hopes with this book is that it creates an urge within you to fight fewer fires and plant more seeds.

So much of this book has been about business. But as a matter of practicality, I figured I would just share a list of some of my very favorite of the actual activities and characteristics of real-life Multipliers that I've incorporated into my own personal life. This is a list of the true "game-changer" activities for me outside of work:

- **Date night:** You have to make your marriage the priority regularly. And if you've never established a dedicated "date night" with your spouse—this will transform your relationship. This is one *weekday* evening where you get a babysitter if you have kids, you turn off your technology and you dedicate some time together to the Significance of your relationship. Spend time getting to know each other. Ask questions about your partner's life and past, as well as his or her future dreams. Develop a genuine curiosity about the person you are spending your life with. I've heard enough stories to realize that divorce is unfortunately a great "un-Multiplier" (or "Divider") of your time and money.

- **Get debt free:** The number one thing that will make you money in your life is your personal income. It's not a get-rich-quick real estate scheme, putting your life savings into a start-up or (initially) learning how to play the stock market. Those are things that might—if you're lucky—make a 10 to 15 percent return for you. What you need first is to get out of debt! Once you're out of debt, your regular income will start piling on top of itself less only what you have in basic on-going monthly bills and taxes. Which means as an investment strategy, getting out of debt is huge because the income you get to keep as a result of being debt free functions *like* the *return* you get on that investment. So since you get to keep something like 80 percent of your earnings by being debt free, it amounts to an 80 percent return on your money! If you make fifty thousand dollars a year (after taxes), then getting to keep forty thousand of it because you don't have debt is much better (not to mention it's guaranteed) than risking ten or twelve thousand on a side real estate project or start-up venture. If you haven't already, go buy Dave Ramsey's book *The Total Money Makeover* and follow it! Paying off my fifty thousand dollars of personal debt was one of the single greatest Multipliers in my life.

- **Stay healthy:** If *multiplying* your time is spending time on things today that create more time tomorrow, then what could be a more directly obvious application of the principle than staying healthy! Give yourself permission to sleep! Harvard Medical School reports that sleep deprivation costs U.S. companies $63.2 billion a year in lost productivity.* And give yourself permission to invest time and money into eating healthier now so that you don't spend time and money trying to get your health back later. The few extra pennies and few extra minutes for "real" food will *multiply* the number of days you have on this earth! Anything that destroys your body reduces your time—don't be stupid.

- Training and personal development: People who say, "I don't have time to read books, go to seminars, get coaching, listen to podcasts" and so on are all mixed up in the mind. Your mind is the most powerful tool you have, but it's only as capable as what you *invest* in it. Multipliers take personal development *very* seriously and it seems to work, so I'm with them! Companies who say, "We don't have time or money to train our people" are just as insane. They are always afraid, saying, "What if we train them and they leave?" But the only thing that will cost you more is what if you *don't* train them and they stay! (Obviously, if it's coaching, consulting or speaking, we can help you with that. For a free introduction to us, visit roryvaden.com.)

- Media: While many people have a love/hate relationship with media, it can be a real Multiplier. It is a blessing to have anyone with a TV show, radio show, blog, podcast, Facebook feed or Twitter stream share your message with their audience. There has never been a time in history where you have

---

*"Time Management Statistics," Key Organization Systems, keyorganization
.com/time-management-statistics.php.

so much access to so many people who can instantly *multiply* your message by sharing it with their audience, or an easier time to create your own media audience. Many of our clients recently have asked us to help them create books as well, since there is something magical about the way a book *multiplies* your influence. There is a guy named Jay Baer who has a superb philosophy and book on creating media called *Youtility*.

- **Infusionsoft:** It's worth mentioning again: If you are a small business, I strongly suggest you check it out. It is incredible how it lets you access all the tools of technology to *multiply* your business without having to be a super tech person. This is another thing that has changed my life. (Learn more at infusionsoft.roryvaden.com.)

- **Treating people right:** To the extent possible, have amazing customer service. It's a Multiplier because it is the source of word of mouth. John DiJulius has written a book called *Secret Service: Hidden Systems That Deliver Unforgettable Customer Service*, which is incredible for this. In general, though, being nice to everyone has been something I learned early on that has worked out well as a Multiplier for me. As it turns out, *everyone* has the VIP hookup somewhere!

- **Integrity:** There is no limit or measure to the incredible *multiplying* effect that your integrity has on everything you do. When you have strong congruence between your words and your actions, people know that what you say is real and they go miles out of their way to help you. When you don't do what you say you're going to do, they want no part of you. If this is something you struggle with—and there was a time in my own life that I did—you need to fix this pretty close to first. I'd suggest getting a copy of my first book, *Take the Stairs*.

- **Faith:** Faith is choosing to trust that what is happening now is for a greater glory later on. That kind of faith gives you protection in times of fear, peace in times of frustration and perspective in times of failure. Faith enables you to see the long term and believe that the things you choose today will ultimately matter and change the course of tomorrow. It is impossible to *multiply* your time without faith because it is predicated upon your believing that your choices now will create a better tomorrow.

- **Good early decisions:** This is one thing that not enough people talk about. It seems that there is the same compounding effect on choices that there is on money. Therefore, I believe that the younger you are, the more amplified your choices are. A young person who makes good decisions repeatedly is going to see their influence, wealth, love and abundance in general multiply. If more young people understood this, then perhaps they would make better choices. I highly recommend that if you are or you know a college-aged student, you at least take the time to hear the details about the Southwestern Advantage summer program. You can do that at swadvantage.roryvaden.com.

Last but not least, it's *people*. Production multiplies most powerfully through people because any one person whom you take an interest in can be the next great Multiplier. Anything that I've done or contrib-

> *Production multiplies most powerfully through people.*

uted to anyone has been the direct result of having been *invested* in by so many others. I'd bet the same is true for you.

The call for each of us, then, should be to choose wisely some people whom we can *invest* in, knowing that they will be the Seed Planters of the future. And our reward is seeing how the things that we have shared with them end up impacting their life in a positive way. There isn't much that is more Significant than that. As mega-Multiplier and Southwestern legend Spencer Hays always says, "You can't build a business; you build people and people build the business."

What is the one thing that all the items in this list have in common?

Simple.

Every single one of them is not a *spending* of time; they are an *investing* of time. Which is ultimately the core of what we've been talking about and gives us cause to make a slightly modified final statement of the message of this entire book:

Multiply your time by giving yourself the emotional *permission* to *invest* time into things today that will create more time and more results for tomorrow.

It reminds me of an old story . . .

A master once called on his workers and delivered some of his gifts to them. To one, he gave five talents. To another he gave two. And to the third he gave one. He had chosen the gifts to reflect each worker's abilities.

The master then went on a journey.

The man who had received five talents traded with them, and made another five talents.

Similarly, the man who had received two talents had also gained two more.

But the man who had received one talent dug a hole into the ground and hid the gift for safekeeping.

When the master returned, he visited the workers to see how they had progressed.

The man who had been given five talents said, "Master, you delivered to me five talents and look! I have gained five more talents in addition to them."

The master said, "Well done. I will make you a ruler over many things."

The man who had been given two talents said, "Master, you delivered to me two talents and look! I have gained two more talents in addition to them."

The master said to him, "Well done. I will make you a ruler over many things."

Then the man who had been given one talent came and said "Master, I was afraid and went and hid your talent in the ground. Look, here you have back what is yours."

The master responded with great dismay, explaining that the talents had been given not to be stowed away for safekeeping, but to be nurtured, shared and multiplied for the benefit of not just the individual who had received them, but of the community as a whole.

The master instructed, "Please hand your talent over to the man who has ten talents. Everyone who has done well with what he has been given will be rewarded with abundance, and those who have not must now learn, the hard way, the lesson that our gifts are meant to be shared."

There is a great lesson that I take from that story as it relates to time:

It is of course not good to waste our time.

But it is also not good enough to *merely* spend our time.

Instead, we must *invest* our time because, out of what's been given to us, we should create for others.

> *We must* invest *our time because, out of what's been given to us, we should create for others.*

Now that you've seen the power of Significance and *multiplication*, you know that the greatest costs are not the ones that are seen; they are the ones that are unseen.

But it is also true that the greatest opportunities have not yet been seen; they remain to be seen.

Just reading this book has cost you something great. As you now know, it was not only the cost printed on the cover of this book, but it was the Significant time that you spent reading it—and all the things you could have been doing instead.

My prayer is that the time you and I have spent together turns out to be a worthwhile investment for you, for those you love and for those things you care most deeply about.

If you believe that it has been, then please *multiply* your impact and mine by telling someone else about the power of this book and the principles inside.

See you in the "stairwell."

ACKNOWLEDGMENTS

Production multiplies most powerfully through people, and you do not complete a work of this magnitude all by yourself. As I look back on my life, it becomes obvious to me that I am the product of so many different people who have invested in me. I hope you will find this book as honoring of you.

First and foremost, thank you to the team at Southwestern Consulting. Our vision of "being the best company in the world at helping people develop the skills and the character they need to achieve their goals in life" is what inspires me each and every day. Your dedication to improving the lives of our clients is rare. It's hard to believe that just a few years ago, there were four of us and now there are too many to list. You truly are a growing army of "Servant Sellers" and it's an honor to be associated with you. You are the Multipliers of the Multipliers.

Thank you to all of the nearly three thousand clients who have taken a chance on partnering with us one-on-one in our coaching program. Getting the chance to work with real people like you on a daily basis for months at a time is what gives our content so much depth. It is a joy and a privilege to struggle through your challenges with you, since it helps us all be better and deliver a better message to the world. We are committed to continually finding ways to help you better achieve your goals in life!

To the team that assembled this book . . . Marian, thank you for your brilliance of always making me sound better and drawing the best out of me. John and the rest of the team at Perigee, thank you for aligning all of your resources in the direction of helping us partner together to make this project successful. Thank you to the team of critical readers who gave me feedback on the early manuscripts: Tim Thomas, Robert Pagliarini, Jason and Denise Dorsey, Lars Tewes, Dustin Hillis, Amanda Vaden and Ellen Petrillo. A special thank-you to Troy Peple: You challenged my thinking, and your honesty helped me reshape an entire third of this book. And of course to Nena—had you not believed in me that fateful day many years ago, this book would not exist.

Thank you to all the Multipliers in this book for allowing us to profile you: Tracy Christman, Pete Wilson, Ron Lamb, Scott Bormann, Troy Peple, Michael Book, Tonya Mayer and Steve Adams. You are all people whom I admire tremendously and whom I consider myself blessed to have worked with. May your example continue to multiply for years to come.

Eric Chester, David Avrin, Jason Dorsey, Jay Baer, Robert D. Smith, and John DiJulius, thank you for your advice and counsel. While you are colleagues I admire who show me what true class looks like in this profession, you are first and foremost friends whom I trust. To Hank, who coached me to have the courage to speak from the heart, share my struggles, and deliver my honest opinions and original thinking—you've made me better.

To Mom, Dad, Randy, Jason and Amanda, thank you for being the most supportive family anyone could ever ask for. To all my friends and family, thank you for investing in me and for giving me the flexibility to invest my time in others and in projects like this book. Special thanks also to my student manager at Southwestern Advantage, Tracey Johnson: If you had never talked to me about selling books door to door then I may never have paid my way through college and I may never have met all the people that have helped me to do what I do—your impact is significant and my love and appreciation for you runs deep!

To the late Dr. Stephen Covey, thank you for your seminal work that redefined the way the world thought about time. Had it not been for you and your team, the thinking laid out in this book may have never developed. And thank you to all those writers and researchers who have helped us try to develop frameworks for thinking about time, your efforts have helped shape my thinking. And I hope that you will find this book uplifting and forwarding to all that you have done. David Allen, Gary Keller, Laura Stack, Kimberly Medlock and Timothy Ferriss are but a few of the thinkers that have influenced me.

Last but not least to my wifey. You are my best friend, my business partner and my soul mate. You bring color to my life and joy to everything that we do together. I admire you, I look up to you, I adore you and I am so so thankful for you. Thank you not only for supporting me but for partnering with me to make a meaningful mark on the world.

God, please use me each day.

Make me a steward of the resources you've given me.

A fiduciary of the skills you've blessed me with.

A conduit for your message to pass.

ABOUT THE AUTHOR

"Self-Discipline Strategist" **Rory Vaden**, MBA, speaks to audiences around the world about how they can leverage self-discipline to achieve their goals in life. His first book, *Take the Stairs*, is a number one *Wall Street Journal* and *USA Today*, as well as a number two *New York Times* bestseller that has been translated into eleven different languages.

As an entrepreneur, he is the cofounder of Southwestern Consulting, a multimillion-dollar global consulting practice with more than seventy team members that helps clients in more than twenty-seven countries to grow their business and provide a better customer experience. Through a proprietary system of utilizing relevant data and time-tested principles, and implementing sales techniques that have been refined over a hundred and fifty years by their parent company, the Southwestern Company, the team can teach anyone with a product or service how to sell more.

Rory's insights on overcoming procrastination, improving self-discipline and increasing productivity have been featured on Fox & Friends, Oprah Radio, CNN and in *Fast Company*, *Entrepreneur*, *Forbes*, *Inc.*, *Success* magazine and many other media outlets. His articles and insights average more than two million views every month, and he is the weekly host of a top twenty-five business news podcast called "Daily Discipline with Rory Vaden."

As a professional speaker, he speaks more than fifty times a year for some of America's best and brightest organizations including: Cargill, the Million Dollar Roundtable, Procter & Gamble, MassMutual, True Value, Young Presidents' Organization, Wells Fargo Advisors, Merck, Land O'Lakes, Novartis and hundreds more. Rory shares ideas for how to grow your sales, increase your self-discipline and get better control of your time so you can serve more people and make more money!

Register for a free call with one of our Southwestern Consulting certified coaches, and/or inquire about having one of our consultants out to your office to do a complimentary one-hour sales training by visiting coaching.roryvaden.com.

Check Rory's availability to speak to your group, connect with his social media profiles, subscribe to his weekly podcast and get more sales insights and inspiration all for free at roryvadenblog.com.